EMBRACING THE INCONCEIVABLE

EMBRACING
THE INCONCEIVABLE

✳

Interspiritual Practice of
Zen and Christianity

Ellen Birx

ORBIS BOOKS
Maryknoll, New York 10545

ORBIS BOOKS
www.orbisbooks.com

Fathers and Brothers
MARYKNOLL™

Founded in 1970, Orbis Books endeavors to publish works that enlighten the mind, nourish the spirit, and challenge the conscience. The publishing arm of the Maryknoll Fathers and Brothers, Orbis seeks to explore the global dimensions of the Christian faith and mission, to invite dialogue with diverse cultures and religious traditions, and to serve the cause of reconciliation and peace. The books published reflect the views of their authors and do not represent the official position of the Maryknoll Society. To learn more about Maryknoll and Orbis Books, please visit our website at www.maryknollsociety.org.

Copyright © 2020 by Ellen Birx

Published by Orbis Books, Box 302, Maryknoll, NY 10545-0302.

The Scripture quotations contained herein are from the New Revised Standard Version Bible, Copyright © 1989, Division of Christian Education of the National Council of the Churches of Christ in the USA. Used by permission. All rights reserved. Hymns cited are in the public domain; lyrics are available at https://hymnary.org.

Manufactured in the United States of America

Library of Congress Cataloging-in-Publication Data

Names: Birx, Ellen, author.
Title: Embracing the inconceivable : interspiritual practice of Zen and
  Christianity / Ellen Birx.
Description: Maryknoll, New York : Orbis Books, [2020] | Includes
  bibliographical references and index. | Summary: "A highly readable
  guide for Christians who are interested in or already engaged in the
  interspiritual practice of Christianity and eastern forms of meditation
  and mindfulness"— Provided by publisher.
Identifiers: LCCN 2019035897 (print) | LCCN 2019035898 (ebook) |
  ISBN 9781626983694 (paperback) | ISBN 9781608338337 (ebook)
Subjects: LCSH: Zen Buddhism—Relations—Christianity. | Christianity and
  other religions—Zen Buddhism. | Spiritual life—Zen Buddhism. |
  Spiritual life—Christianity.
Classification: LCC BQ9269.4.C5 B57 2020 (print) | LCC BQ9269.4.C5
  (ebook) | DDC 261.2/43927—dc23
LC record available at https://lccn.loc.gov/2019035897
LC ebook record available at https://lccn.loc.gov/2019035898

To my teacher Roshi Robert Jinsen Kennedy, S.J.,
and my teacher's teacher Roshi Bernie Tetsugen Glassman
with unbounded love and gratitude

Contents

Part III. Discovering the Nonseparate Self

Part IV. Meditating and Praying

Part V. Embodying Loving Action

Preface

"Are we one or are we not?" This is the challenge Roshi Bernie
Glassman put forth in a booming voice to his Zen community
amid the din of dismay and disapproval that erupted when he
announced that he planned to authorize a Jesuit priest, Robert
Kennedy, as a Zen teacher. How can a non-Buddhist, a Christian
no less, be a fully authorized Zen teacher? Bernie was not one to
be boxed in by narrow beliefs or by imaginary boundaries and
barriers. He had a broad vision and a deep sense of the oneness
of life. Throughout his life, he honored both his Jewish heritage
and his Zen insights. He felt that people of any faith, or none, can
benefit from Zen practice and from the realization of our oneness
with ultimate reality, God, the earth, and each other.

Since I am a dharma successor of Roshi Robert Kennedy, Bernie is my Zen grandfather. This book honors Bernie's vision to
share Zen beyond the bounds of Buddhism. It serves as a guide
for people practicing in more than one faith and as a help to
people raised in a Judeo-Christian culture who are trying to integrate their religion of birth with their chosen practice of Zen or
other forms of meditation. In my life, the practice of Zen and the
practice of Christianity have been mutually enriching. Hopefully,
this book frees readers to practice across religious boundaries,

appreciating the differences among traditions while simultaneously experiencing that, ultimately, *we are one.*

Back in the 1980s, Bernie came to visit Sisters of Saint Joseph
of Peace Janet Richardson, Rosalie McQuaide, and Mary Byrnes,
who lived in Jersey City. These three sisters had practiced Zen
meditation and had attended many of Bernie's *sesshins*, silent Zen
meditation retreats, for years. Zen typically does not use the word
god because of the baggage the name carries as an anthropomorphic, personal creator, yet as Bernie visited with the nuns, he
heard them frequently mention God. Bernie said that the thought
popped into his mind, *After all these years of Zen practice, why
are these nuns still talking about God?* In a flash it came to him,
*Why not? If I really believe in "not knowing" and I'm open to all
possibilities, why not?* Bernie said this was a pivotal moment of
insight for him.

Throughout this book I use typical Zen words for the highest
reality, such as *ultimate reality, the absolute, emptiness,* and *thusness.* I also use the Judeo-Christian word *God.* I encourage you,
the reader, to choose whatever words are most helpful to you.

Acknowledgments

I thank my husband, Charles, who has been my spiritual companion for more than fifty years. He read the manuscript several times and offered many helpful suggestions at each stage of its development.

Many thanks to my daughter, Clare; her husband, Troy; and my granddaughters, Brenna and Elise, who provided me with wonderful entertainment and refreshing breaks from writing. Thanks also to my grandson, Matt, and his new wife, Mairead, who were married during the writing of this book. My family keeps me in touch with my playful side and with the language and culture of younger generations.

I bow in gratitude to my Zen teacher, Roshi Robert Kennedy, SJ; my teacher's teacher, Roshi Bernie Glassman; and all Zen teachers and practitioners back to Buddha who kept this practice alive to this day. This includes all the members of New River Zen Community who keep Zen fresh and vital in the mountains of southwestern Virginia.

Deep gratitude to my Christian community, near and far, especially Jan Hencke; Rosemary O'Connell; Amy Yee; Roshi Ruben Habito; Sensei Barbara Craig, RSM; Sensei Rosalie McQuaide, CSJP; Roshi Janet Richardson, CSJP; Reverend Michael Holleran,

Sensei; and Reverend Monica Maher, Sensei. They are shining examples of interspiritual practice.

Special thanks to Jill O'Brien and the team at Orbis Books who supported this book and made it a reality. Finally, I thank Paul McMahon, whose excellent editing refined this book.

Part I

Entering Interspiritual Practice

1

Zen and Nonduality

The word *Zen* has come into common usage in our culture to mean a calm, serene state of body and mind. For many people, Zen conjures up the image of a meticulously landscaped garden, its simplicity accentuating the natural beauty of each rock, tree, and blossom. Advertisements for Zen spas, Zen restaurants, and Zen decor attempt to convey the message that you will experience a calm, relaxed state of mind if you use these products. While Zen certainly relieves stress and promotes equanimity, Zen is so much more.

Zen is a simple, yet profound path of meditation that is concerned with the realization of ultimate reality and the direct experience of nonduality. Zen is a twenty-five-hundred-year-old tradition originating with Buddha in India. Indian Buddhism migrated into China, where it was influenced by Taoism and Confucianism and emerged as Chan, which is the Chinese word for Zen. It then made its way to Japan, Korea, and Vietnam. Zen is now practiced in countries around the world, where it mixes and mingles with the local culture. This book describes a continuation of that process in America as Zen influences and is influenced by our scientific and predominantly Judeo-Christian culture.

Some Zen terminology, such as *nonduality*, can seem abstract and confusing. However, before I was a nurse, a nursing professor, or a Zen teacher, I was a first-grade teacher, so I am confident that I can make Zen terms clear and simple. The word *nondual* simply means "not two." It refers to the physical and spiritual aspects of life being not two. They are not separate. They are two aspects of each person or thing, two aspects of the whole. Nonduality is seeing beyond your sense of a separate self to experience that you are not separate from ultimate reality, the universe, other people, or life itself.

Whether we are children or adults, we learn best by doing, so in addition to reading this book, I encourage you to meditate daily. Instructions for Zen meditation appear in chapter 3. Zen is a path of meditation. Nonduality is not a term to be defined and comprehended by the intellect, but rather an experience that you can cultivate through meditation. Nonduality is a spiritual experience that involves the whole person—body, mind, heart, and spirit. This book provides a map of the territory, but while a map is helpful, it is not the experience itself. Meditation is a way to take the journey, grow in awareness, and experience for yourself.

When my brothers and sisters and I were kids, lined up in the backseat of the car during a family vacation, our parents would get upset if they turned to see us sleeping or reading a comic book. Those were the old days. Now kids sit in the backseat watching movies or fiddling with their smartphones, and as long as they are entertaining themselves and not bothering anyone else, nobody cares. However, my parents would say, "Put the comic book down. Sit up and look at the scenery. You can sleep or read comics when we get home. You are missing seeing something new. You might learn something." We would begrudgingly sit up, put the comic books away, and look out the window for a while. We did expand our horizons by seeing the Adirondack Mountains, the Rocky Mountains, and even the seemingly endless cornfields of Nebraska. We learned that the country is much bigger than we imagined.

Meditation is a way to sit up, let go of your usual distractions, pay attention, and experience something new. It is not a time to sleep or entertain yourself with daydreams, stories, or mental commentaries. This place, this moment, is the destination. In the silent stillness of meditation, you can see, hear, and feel the subtle, spiritual aspect of all phenomena and the underlying unity of life itself comes to the fore.

Zen is not the only path through the nondual spiritual terrain, but the Zen path of meditation is the one with which I am intimately familiar, and is the focus of this book. Brother Wayne Teasdale, who coined the term *interspirituality*, describes it as "the sharing of ultimate experiences across traditions" (Teasdale 1999, 26). For me, interspirituality takes the form of practicing both Zen and Christianity as mutually enriching spiritual traditions. However, what follows may be relevant and helpful to people engaged in other forms of interspiritual practice.

We live in a world that is out of balance with greed and materialism running rampant to the point of ecological crisis. Our scientific age yields immense knowledge about the physical world that has the potential to improve the quality of life on our planet. However, scientific knowledge alone is not enough. It needs to be integrated with spiritual wisdom to restore balance, decrease suffering, and avert disaster. The point of Zen meditation is to experience ultimate reality directly and awaken to the spiritual wisdom needed to live a full, balanced, and compassionate life.

There is more to life than the material world. As human beings we can sense that we are each more than a physical body made up of numerous parts. We are thinking, feeling, storytelling beings who reflect on our experiences. Some of us sense that we are more than physical and psychological beings. We have a sense of the sacred; we are also spiritual beings.

Zen meditation is a way to expand our worldview beyond a materialistic, cause-and-effect approach to realize a nondual approach that does not separate the spiritual from the physical aspects of reality. A nondual approach requires more than logic and intellect. You can understand nonduality intellectually to some extent, but an intellectual understanding alone will not transform your life. Just as the scientific research process is used to discover and generate scientific knowledge, meditation is a process that opens us to nondual insight and spiritual wisdom.

A classic Zen chant, the *Heart Sutra*, contains a line that says, "Form is no other than emptiness; emptiness no other than form" (*Zen Peacemaker Order Service Book* 1997, 4). *Form* means all the things in the universe, such as stars, planets, rocks, water, people, animals, and cars. It also refers to mental forms such as thoughts, concepts, theories, stories, opinions, emotions, and images.

Emptiness is a Zen term referring to that which is formless, that which is empty of substance and boundaries. Other names for emptiness are *ultimate reality*, the *absolute*, or the *infinite*. Form is finite; the formless is infinite. The finite can be measured; the infinite is immeasurable. Emptiness refers to the spiritual aspect of each thing, each person, the universe, the totality, the indivisible whole.

"Form is no other than emptiness; emptiness no other than form" means that form and emptiness are not two separate things. Emptiness or formless ultimate reality takes form. Ultimate reality manifests as everything in the universe. However, form does not exhaust the formless. The formless is greater than form. The infinite includes but exceeds the finite.

Zen does not use the word *god* to refer to the infinite, ineffable, inconceivable highest reality. Zen uses words such as *emptiness, empty oneness, ultimate reality, the absolute, the infinite, thusness, suchness*, or *it*. Zen emphasizes direct experience of the ineffable rather than words or interpretations. The word *god* tends to connote a personal God who created the world. Zen is nontheistic. From a Zen perspective, ultimate reality cannot be described using words like personal or impersonal. Ultimate reality is utterly indescribable. Zen frees us to move beyond either/or thinking. Those of us practicing Zen who grew up with the word *god* and with the experience of a personal relationship with God need not give these up. God is large. God can be called by many names, or by no name, and can be experienced in innumerable ways.

Growing up in a Western culture, I learned as a child that God created the universe and everything in it. Meditation helped me grow beyond a childlike vision of God as a separate being who stood apart and created the universe like a person building a house or a car. I no longer experience human beings as containers into which God pours his spirit. The body, mind, heart, and spirit are one—one manifestation of God. God as the formless infinite or ultimate reality takes form, and everything in the universe is a manifestation or expression of the living God. I encounter each thing and each being as sacred, spiritual, and a way to know God alive in the world today. Zen dissolves even the faintest concept of God, and the living, breathing God comes forth here and now. Zen practice and the direct experience of nonduality continuously open me to new dimensions of the infinite, inconceivable God. This book is for those who yearn for the awe, reverence, and joy of a life not separate from God or the highest reality.

2

My Christian Heritage

I was baptized as an infant at the Presbyterian church that my father's family attended for generations and where my family went to church and Sunday school. My brother, sisters, several neighbor friends, and I also went to vacation Bible school at a small nondenominational church we walked to down the road from where we lived. I remember winning a prize one summer for memorizing the most Bible verses. The prize was a silk scarf with a red border and horses of all kinds scattered in the middle. In sixth grade, I completed confirmation classes at the Presbyterian church and was confirmed.

During the years I was in junior high, a new church formed in our neighborhood that was part of the United Church of Christ. My mother, who was involved in the civil rights movement and the women's movement, felt a match with the views and social action of this congregation, so our family became members of this church. During my junior high and senior high school years, I participated in youth group and social action activities. My husband often teases me to this day that the first time he invited me to go to the movies with him to see *Mary Poppins*, I declined, saying that I couldn't go because I had youth group that evening. My husband and I were married at this church in a lovely candlelight ceremony on a snowy evening in January surrounded by family and friends.

During our college years, we were engaged in various types of social action. We volunteered to work at a migrant day care center near the college. We provided activities for preschool children while their parents worked in the orchards. Memories of two children stayed with us all these years. One was a tiny African American toddler who was exceptionally bright, active, and agile. It was a challenge to keep up with him, but we were energized, charmed, and amazed by his bright eyes and constant curiosity. We have always wondered what became of him and if he got the opportunity to develop his talents. The other child was a severely disabled African American three-year-old who could not walk or speak. He laid on a mat at the edge of the play area, sometimes in a world of his own and sometimes watching the other children playing around the room. We held him, read to him, and sang to him. At the end of the day, we carried him in our arms off the school bus and placed him into the arms of his mother or father waiting to meet the bus at the end of the dirt road leading into the migrant camp. These were the spiritual experiences of our young adult years.

We thought about joining the Peace Corps but wanted to help meet the needs of Native Americans, so as soon as my husband finished his teaching certificate, he applied for a job with the Bureau of Indian Affairs and was assigned to teach at Kaibeto Primary School, forty miles from Tuba City, twenty-two of which were a washboard, dusty dirt road. We poured out our youthful idealism and enthusiasm providing enriching activities for the kids such as picnics, field trips, plays, crafts, Cub Scouts, movie nights, and parties. Some of these events were attended by the whole community—like Thanksgiving dinner—which felt like the first Thanksgiving we learned about as children. We encouraged the children to retain and cherish their Navajo culture and language as they learned English and acquired knowledge and skills that would lead to employment in the future. We learned as much from the children as they did from us. The parents were grateful for the education their children received and invited us to healing ceremonies, called sings, they were having at their hogans out in the surrounding desert. These were interpersonal, intercultural, and interspiritual experiences that showed us how to integrate the best of two worlds.

Within the Navajo reservation is the Hopi reservation. We were invited to attend dances and ceremonies in the Hopi village of Hotevilla. These were adventures into another world and time. On one occasion, we were invited by a Hopi elder named David Mononye to come down into the kiva for a ceremony where Native Americans from various tribes each brought pieces of a stone tablet that were put back together like the pieces of a puzzle and a prophesy written on the tablet was revealed. After some of the ceremonies, David invited us back to his home where we listened to his stories and ate blue piki bread prepared by his wife. One day after several visits to Hotevilla, David explained to us that he felt it was important for white people to understand and respect the Hopi Way, but since we weren't born Hopi, it was not our way. He urged us to return to our own tradition, go deep into it to find what is true and good, and bring that forth to benefit the people and the earth.

It was in this spirit that we turned our attention anew to our own Christian tradition. My husband, Charles, had been raised Catholic, and since Catholicism included a deep contemplative tradition that paralleled our interest in and practice of meditation, we chose to become active in the Catholic Church. Charles attended classes at St. Bernard's Seminary and was ordained a permanent deacon. At that time, wives were encouraged to participate in the diaconal studies and ministries of their husbands, so I attended classes with Charles on Old Testament, New Testament, systematic theology, moral theology, pastoral theology, spiritual formation, and homiletics, although I was not formally enrolled in diaconal studies since women cannot hold such leadership positions in the Catholic Church.

The limited role of women in the Catholic Church eventually led me to return to my Protestant roots. In this regard, I was inspired by my great-great-great-aunt Anna Howard Shaw, who was the first woman in the United States to be ordained a minister in the Methodist Protestant Church. She was a strong, practical woman who grew up in the wilderness of Michigan helping her family clear timber, build a log cabin, grow crops, hunt for food, gather wood, build fires, and survive harsh winters. Her family did not approve of her going to Boston to attend Boston University School of Theology so she nearly starved pursuing this dream on her own. After several years of parish ministry, she returned to Boston University to become a physician and she ministered to the medical needs of people living in poor city neighborhoods. She is best known as a protégée of Susan B. Anthony and an orator for the cause of women's right to vote. Her feminist Christianity, her expansive view of God as "the Infinite," her love for humanity, her service to the poor, and her passion for justice and reform make her an abiding role model and influence in my Christian life.

By happenstance one day in the early 1980s, Charles spotted a flyer on the bulletin board at St. Bernard's Seminary that told about interfaith retreats that were being given by Roshi Bernie Glassman, Rabbi Don Singer, and Father Robert Kennedy at the Zen Community of New York. Roshi Bernie Glassman was involved in starting a bakery where people who were homeless or unemployed could learn job skills and become employed. Charles sought permission from the diaconal program director to spend his summer practicum month at the Zen Community of New York, practicing Zen meditation, engaging in interfaith dialogue, and working in the bakery. The director was a forward-looking man who encouraged the diaconal candidates to be creative in developing new ministries, and he readily approved the proposal, with the condition that Charles have a priest who agreed to supervise his practicum experience. Father Kennedy agreed to serve in this role, and this is where we first met our future Zen teacher.

It is through our decades of interfaith work and Zen practice with Roshi Kennedy that we have been able to go deep enough into our own Christian tradition to bring forth new insights into Christianity, spoken in a language that can reach the hearts and transform the lives of people in the twenty-first century. This book is my response to the urging of Hopi elder David so many years ago.

3

Zen Experience, Christian Experience

Spirituality is not an intellectual pursuit; it is experiential. Reading and thinking about spirituality can only take you so far, and then you need to move beyond the intellect to involve the whole body, heart, hands, and mind.

For thirty-two years I was a nursing professor. One morning each week I taught the students in the classroom and another day each week I took students to the hospital for their clinical practicum. At the hospital, the students applied their knowledge and skills in complex health-care settings providing hands-on care for real human beings with serious illnesses. Clinical experience brought to life what the students learned in class and from their textbooks. Along with gaining critical thinking and technical skills, the students grew in their interpersonal skills and humanity. In interacting with their patients, they came face-to-face with their own strength, fragility, and mortality. It was the experiential learning in a clinical setting and the human-to-human relationships with patients that transformed a student into a competent and caring nurse.

Zen is an experiential spiritual path. The essential aspect of this path is daily sitting meditation, called *zazen*. Many people say they are interested in Zen—they read Zen books, tell Zen stories, and enjoy Zen poetry—but they don't sit down and meditate each day. This is not Zen practice. Zen practice requires the discipline of sitting in zazen each day.

When I instruct someone in how to do zazen, I start out with showing them the posture. With your sit bones on the front of a firm cushion, let your knees open down onto the mat with your feet one in front of the other on the mat in front of the cushion. Called the Burmese meditation position, this forms a stable tripod base for the rest of your body. The natural curve in the lower back is increased slightly to open the abdomen for relaxed, natural abdominal breathing during meditation. You sit up straight, tall, and balanced, not rigid. Your shoulders are down and back, not slumped. Your head is facing straight ahead with your ears over your shoulders. Your eyes are cast downward looking at the floor a couple feet in front of you. Hands are lightly clasped resting in your lap on your upper thighs close to your lower abdomen. This posture can be adapted for people who need to sit on a bench or a chair. The reason so much attention is given to proper posture during zazen is that during zazen you are not just alert and attentive mentally, but with every cell in the body.

During zazen, the attention is on the breath in the abdomen, which naturally expands with inhalation and recedes with exhalation. Don't try to regulate the breath; just be aware of the belly rising and falling with the natural breathing. When the mind wanders off in thought, let go of the thought and bring the attention back to the breathing, just the sensation of the belly rising and falling. When a thought comes, don't try to push it out. Just don't intentionally add to it. When you notice you are mentally replaying a situation that happened during the day, don't choose to stay with that situation. Let go of the thoughts about the situation and bring the attention back to just breathing. Each time you notice that your mind has wandered, it is an opportunity to choose to let go of the thought and return your attention to the breathing. Zazen is a time set aside to take a break from your usual thinking, daydreaming, problem solving, and mental commentary. In the silence and stillness of zazen you can open to something new.

In his book *Zen: The Authentic Gate*, Yamada Roshi discusses five phases of religious life: belief, understanding, practice, realization, and actualization (Yamada 2015, 11). The first two, belief and understanding, he categorizes as faith-based spirituality. Practice, realization, and actualization are categorized as experience-based spirituality. Many people go no further than belief and understanding, and they are left with a spirituality that is primarily intellectual.

Zen begins with the belief that Buddha and the long tradition of Zen teachers and practitioners who followed him saw something through meditation that is worthwhile in reducing human suffering and liberating the human spirit. Understanding is gained through reading, chanting sutras, and listening to talks by Zen teachers. However, from the start, the emphasis is on direct experience gained through the regular practice of meditation. Realization and insights gained through meditation are applied in daily life. This is called *actualization*. A person can have a flash of insight, but the challenge of refining the character to respond appropriately and compassionately in each situation that presents itself is the work of a lifetime.

Many people view Christianity as primarily a faith-based religion rooted in belief and understanding gained through reading the Bible and attending church and Sunday school. However, many Christians today and through the ages have practiced prayer, contemplation, and works of charity and have had a wide variety of religious experiences. Many sought to actualize their Christian experiences in the way they lived their life through kindness and compassionate action.

Christian realization or awakening, sometimes called being born again, is the experience of God's unconditional love, not only that you are loved completely just as you are, but that you are an expression of God's love and have the capacity to share that love with others. Being a Christian begins with belief in what Jesus taught about a loving God. Our understanding grows by reading in the Bible about how Jesus lived his life in a way that was inclusive, healing, and loving. But this is just the beginning of Christian spirituality. Through the practice of prayer, participation in the Christian community, and acts of loving service to others, the heart is opened to the direct experience of God's love. Experiencing God's love is not a matter of intellectual understanding; it is an experience of the heart, of the whole person.

As a teenager, you hear about people falling in love. You read books and watch movies about it and hope that the right person will come along, and it will happen for you one day. But it is always a surprise when it actually happens; you are caught off guard by how your life changes overnight. The experience of God's love is different from falling in love with a person, but it is no less dramatic or life-changing.

Throughout my life I was open to God and experienced God's love in various ways. However, when I was in my mid-twenties and living in Dallas, Texas, I was surrounded by Christians who were more expressive about their Christianity and more evangelical than those I had known earlier in my life. One day I decided to pray as they did, surrendering myself to Jesus, asking him to come into my heart, and making a commitment to follow Jesus in the way I lived my life. I immediately felt God's abundant and unconditional love wash over and through me, permeating every cell in my body and every corner of my heart and mind. I felt known and loved completely just as I was. I clearly "heard" the words, "You are mine, but don't stop sitting." I was surprised by the words "You are mine." It wasn't something I would be likely to say or think. I was equally surprised when I later came across these words in Isaiah 43:1.

The words "but don't stop sitting" were a deeply felt calling to me. At that time, I had been meditating every day for several years, and although this wasn't the usual practice for Christians back in the 1970s, it was a major aspect of my spiritual life. In my heart, these words meant that meditation was a valuable gift to humankind that I should continue to nurture, and I did. For me, meditation was a way to answer the great commandment of Jesus to "Love the Lord your God with all your heart, and with all your soul, and with all your mind, and with all your strength"

(Mark 12:30) by dedicating time each day to sit silently in God's presence. The rest of the great commandment is to love others as yourself. It was at this time that I returned to school to become a nurse, viewing this work as an act of love and service to others.

Simultaneously, I practiced Christianity and Zen. Zen practice opens a person to a particular kind of insight or awakening experience that is sometimes called *kenshō*. Zen insights are not like psychological insights that one might have through psychotherapy. Zen insights are direct experiences of the emptiness of all phenomena including yourself. The experience of emptiness defies description or explanation. The experience is unique for each person, but it liberates each person from the sense of being a separate self. There is no separation from the world around you. This shift in the way a person experiences him- or herself, others, the universe, and ultimate reality often includes the experience that in empty oneness there are no boundaries between inside and outside, no subject-object duality, and the limits of time and space are transcended.

After many years of zazen, early one morning while attending a Zen retreat in Boulder, Colorado, I was blessed to have such an experience. I awoke before dawn with a sense of anxiety or tension in my abdomen and decided to lay quietly in bed and let my attention be with the sensation. As I did this, almost immediately, it was as if the vast sky opened and there was no separate me. I was one with the Flatirons and the whole Rocky Mountain Range. In this empty oneness, space and time collapsed and I was not separate from the moon and the farthest star. My description does not do the experience justice, nor does it adequately convey the lasting impact it has had on my life.

The intensity of this experience was amazing and lasted for about a month, but the shift in my perception of emptiness—myself as not separate, and oneness with people and everything I see—stayed with me to this day. Once I saw the empty oneness of everything, including myself, I could never not see it. A separate, isolated self simply does not exist.

This Zen awakening experience did not negate my previous Christian awakening to God's love; it expanded it. Now it was not me loving God, or God loving me, but one infinite love, God's love, with no separation whatsoever. I now experienced myself as a manifestation of God. Infinite ultimate reality, which I call God, is greater than me—immanent in me, others, and the world—but also transcendent, inconceivable, and inexhaustible.

My Christian experiences and my Zen experiences are different, but they do not contradict each other. They are complementary and mutually enriching. The one infinite God is multifaceted and can be experienced in many ways.

Part II

Experiencing Nondual Spirituality

4

Ultimate Reality and a Nondual God

Zen doesn't use the word god, but it is certainly concerned with realizing ultimate reality. Zen is not simply the pursuit of relaxation and focus; it is opening to that which is beyond all words and concepts. Because Zen and Buddhism don't use the word god, many people conclude that they are atheistic, but this is not the case. They do not assert that there is no God, but rather that ultimate reality is beyond dualistic divisions. Ultimate reality is not separate from creation, the universe, or this very earth. Everything is a manifestation or the functioning of ultimate reality. Sometimes the name, the great functioning, is used to indicate ultimate reality that is not separate from all that we see or from life itself. Yet ultimate reality is not limited to creation or the universe.

Sometimes the term panentheistic has been applied to Zen and Buddhism. This term may be useful in that in indicates that ultimate reality manifests in everything and yet is greater than the sum of everything in the universe. However, panentheistic is not completely accurate in that it brings in the idea of theism to categorize a completely different view of reality. The term nontheistic is also used sometimes to describe Zen and Buddhism because it denotes a view of ultimate reality that is not a personal, creator God like the God of Judaism, Christianity, and Islam. However, the term nontheistic does not mean that Zen and Buddhism are not concerned with ultimate reality. It means ultimate reality transcends all theologies.

What is important in Zen is not philosophical labels or comparisons with other religious views, but rather the direct experience of ultimate reality encountered through the silence and stillness of meditation. When the mind is not distracted by discursive thought, and our constant labeling and categorizing, ultimate reality beyond thoughts and concepts is revealed. It is already here; we simply awaken to it.

As a person with a deep experience of God in my life prior to beginning Zen practice, the Zen experience of ultimate reality beyond thoughts and concepts opened me to a larger God. It did not require me to stop using the word God; it expanded my experience of God beyond the boundaries of space, time, and words of any kind. Most importantly, I experienced that there is no self at all apart from ultimate reality. There are no subjects or objects, just the functioning of ultimate reality.

After the Zen experience of awakening to ultimate reality and the ongoing deepening of this experience, the words of Jesus expressing nonduality became clear and alive for me. Jesus said, "The Father and I are one" (John 10:30). This statement is not true just for Jesus; it is true for each of us. Jesus prayed for his disciples "that they may be one, as we are one, I in them and you in me, that they may become completely one" (John 17:22–23). We are already one, but we need to become aware of this oneness. Essential in both Zen and Christianity is the realization of our true identity in oneness with ultimate reality or God.

Jesus was accused of blasphemy for saying that he, as a human being, was one with God. He was not saying that he or other humans, such as the disciples, were the same as or equal to God. He was expressing the fundamental unity or oneness of God and all of God's creation. God is greater than the total of all creation and at the same time is not other than creation nor separate from it.

This principle of distinct but not separate is important in both Buddhism and Christianity. In his book *Zen for Americans*, Zen Master Soyen Shaku emphasizes that the Buddhist conception of ultimate reality or God includes both the gate of sameness and the gate of difference. The gate of sameness refers to ultimate reality, or God, and the gate of difference refers to ultimate reality or God manifesting in this world. Ultimate reality, or God, is "the One," and this world of individuals and things is "the Many." Shaku states, "Things are many and yet one; they are one and yet many. I am not thou, and thou are not I; and yet we are all one in essence" (1906/1987, 127).

In ancient times Zen Master Dongshan Liangjie was walking through the woods, and when he crossed a mountain stream he saw his reflection in the water and was suddenly awakened. He expressed his insight in verse:

> Avoid seeking Him in someone else
> Or you will be far apart from the self.
> Solitary now am I, and independent,
> But I meet Him everywhere.
> He now is surely me,
> But I am not Him.
> Understanding it in this way,
> You will directly be one with thusness. (Cook 2003, 197)

Dongshan Liangjie experienced his true identity as ultimate reality functioning in this world, but also acknowledged that neither he nor everything else in the world exhausts ultimate reality. Ultimate reality is the underlying oneness of the world and at the same time is greater than the world. The One manifesting in each of us and in each particular thing, just as it is, is expressed using the word thusness rather than the word god.

Although the words used are different, Dongshan Liangjie's verse clarifies what Jesus meant when he said, "The Father and I are one" (John 10:30). Jesus told the disciples, "Whoever has seen me has seen the Father" (John 14:9). Oneness or nonduality is a major emphasis in the teaching of Jesus. Jesus and the Father are one and yet distinct. Oneness is one side of the coin, and differences or distinctions are the other side of the coin. We acknowledge the oneness but also the distinctions. We are distinct from God but not separate.

One of Jesus's most powerful nondual teachings is when he said, "Truly I tell you, just as you did it to one of the least of these who are members of my family, you did it to me" (Matt. 25:40). This is a clear expression of Jesus's oneness with each person, including those considered least fortunate. It is his clear call to awaken to this oneness and respond with love and compassionate action.

Nonduality comes through clearly in the Last Supper, which Christians around the world celebrate to this day. Jesus took a loaf of bread, blessed it, broke it, and gave it to the disciples saying, "Take, eat; this is my body" (Matt. 26:26). Then he did the same with the wine. In declaring his presence in the bread that we eat and the wine we drink, Jesus proclaimed the oneness of life. Communion is a regular reminder and celebration of the underlying unity and oneness of all of life.

This is similar to the Zen teaching "Pick up the whole earth in your fingers, and it's as big as a grain of rice" (Cleary & Cleary 2005, 31). Ultimate reality, whole and complete, is manifested or expressed in each and every person or thing: a grain of rice, a piece of bread, a sip of wine, or a person considered to be the least in some way. To experience this reality for yourself in your daily life is nonduality.

One evening Ralph, a member of New River Zen Community, gave a Zen talk and told the group how he was an English major back in his college days. He remembered studying the poetry of William Blake. The professor asked the class what Blake meant by his poem that began,

> To see a World in a Grain of Sand
> And a Heaven in a Wild Flower,
> Hold Infinity in the palm of your hand,
> And Eternity in an hour. (Erdman 1982, 490)

Ralph said that he didn't have any idea what it meant nor did anyone else in the class, including the professor. However, he was happy to report that after many years of Zen practice, the meaning is now clear!

5

The Inconceivable

In the Zen tradition, there is an emphasis on not knowing, as exemplified by the famous dialogue between Emperor Wu and Bodhidharma. Emperor Wu asks Bodhidharma, "Who is standing before me?" Bodhidharma replies, "No knowing" (Sekida 2005, 147). This is sometimes translated as "I don't know" (Cleary & Cleary 2005, 1).

Not knowing is not the opposite of knowing. It is not ignorance. It is complete openness to what is right before you, not limited by any concept or thought. Zen urges us to experience that which is beyond knowing and not knowing.

In one of my favorite koans, Zen Master Danxia asked his student Wukong, "What is the Self prior to the empty eon?" Wukong started to say something in reply, but before he could get the words out of his mouth, his teacher hushed him, saying, "You're noisy. Go away for a while." One day, Wukong climbed a mountain and, standing on its peak and looking off in all directions, he was suddenly awakened. He returned to his teacher who acknowledged his awakening and slapped him on the shoulder saying, "I think you know it exists." Wukong bowed joyfully (Cook 2003, 237).

Wukong directly encountered the inconceivable, which is beyond knowing and not knowing. The verse to this koan says,

The icy spring of the valley stream—no one peeks into it.
It does not allow travelers to penetrate its depth. (Cook 2003, 240)

26

We can see and taste the valley stream, but its source remains hidden; its depth is unfathomable.

In the Christian contemplative tradition, we hear a similar teaching in these lines of the poem "The Dark Nights," by St. John of the Cross:

> O guiding night!
> O night more lovely than the dawn!
> O night that has united
> The Lover with His beloved,
> Transforming the beloved in her Lover. (Kavanaugh & Kavanaugh 1979, 69)

The darkness of night is a metaphor for encountering the inconceivable. One must turn to poetry to point toward the ineffable. In this darkness, the Lover and beloved are united, and the beloved is transformed.

In Zen, we are always urged to keep going, deeper and deeper. The *Heart Sutra* culminates in the *prajnaparamita* mantra, which says,

> Gone, gone, gone beyond, gone altogether beyond,
> O what an awakening, all-hail! (Conze 1972, 101–2)

Ultimate reality or emptiness is infinitely subtle, so there is no end to our sitting in meditation to plumb its depths, no end to our journey, no final word of Zen.

In her book *The Flowing Bridge*, Catholic nun and Zen Roshi Elaine MacInnes shared her profound experiences working with the three initial koans in the Sanbo Kyodan lineage of Zen. The first is the well-known koan, Joshu's Mu. This koan helps a Zen practitioner awaken to the emptiness of self and everything in the phenomenal world. This is a transformative awakening to nonseparation or nonduality.

The second koan is Kongen: "What is the root-source of Mu?" This koan is far less well known and rarely mentioned outside private meetings with the Zen teacher. Roshi MacInnes points out that Mu is the root, and Kongen refers to the source. She says, "Having come to the knowing of the root, one comes to the not-knowing of the source" (MacInnes 2007, 13). Kongen invites the practitioner to enter deeply, right through the heart of Mu, going utterly beyond, to encounter the inconceivable, indescribable mystery at its core. Roshi MacInnes says, "Kongen is the unutterable inconceivability of God" (2007, 15).

In encountering the inconceivable, you discover that you also are inconceivable. It's not simply that you are inconceivable, but that what you are capable of is also inconceivable. With this realization, you bow in gratitude to the inconceivable and honor the call to share your gifts and capabilities for the well-being of the earth and all beings. It is in coming face-to-face with the great mystery that the Zen experience and the Christian experience coincide most closely. It is in living out this wisdom in a life of compassionate action that they walk hand in hand.

The third koan is the famous "What is the sound of one hand?" This koan awakens the practitioner to experiencing everything in the universe, including oneself, as the manifestation of inconceivable ultimate reality or God. This is not a concept. It is experienced as *the fact*. This brings incredible beauty and freshness to life. The song of the inconceivable reverberates everywhere. This insight brings immeasurable joy, energy, peace, and love to share with those we meet.

Christian theologian Roger Haight describes the core of Christian faith as relationship with God, who is personal, loving, and present to all, as revealed through Jesus's life and teachings. At the same time, God is "infinite, unimaginable, and incomprehensible reality; in short, God is absolute mystery" (Haight 2016, 167).

As a Christian I know God through the life and teachings of Jesus and as the risen Christ manifesting in the world today. At the same time, the Christian tradition acknowledges the incomprehensible, inconceivable mystery of God. Knowing God intimately and not knowing the inconceivable God are both embraced. For me, Zen is a contemplative path leading straight into the heart of inconceivable mystery where my faith is expanded, enriched, and transformed. I share the prayer of Paul, "To know the love of Christ that surpasses knowledge, so that you [we] may be filled with all the fullness of God" (Eph. 4:10).

The Zen tradition expresses both knowing and not knowing in the following verse from *The Record of Transmitting the Light*:

> The moonlight reflected in the bottom of the pond is bright
>   in the sky;
> The water reaching to the sky is totally clear and pure.
> Though you scoop it up repeatedly and try to know it,
> Vast, clarifying all, it remains unknown. (Cook 2003, 146)

Although the moonlight of ultimate reality, or ultimate mystery, clarifies everything and makes all things known, ultimate reality itself cannot be grasped with the intellect or imagination. It remains unknown and inconceivable. Ultimate reality is the great mystery that is functioning in this world, in ourselves, and in all that we see extending out to the ends of the universe and beyond. In this great mystery, we are united and at the same time the subtle moonlight accentuates the inconceivable uniqueness of each thing or person we behold.

In the *Heart Sutra* we chant,

> No eye, ear, nose, tongue, body, mind;
> No color, sound, smell, taste, touch, thing;
> No realm of sight, no realm of consciousness. (*Zen Peacemaker Order Service Book* 1997, 4)

We are urged to go beyond anything we can perceive by the senses, mind, or consciousness. In a similar way, we hear in

Christian Scripture, "No eye has seen, nor ear heard, nor human heart conceived, what God has prepared for those who love him" (1 Cor. 2:9). Here too we must go beyond what the senses can perceive or what the human heart can conceive. Ultimately it is the inconceivable mystery realizing itself. This is the spiritual practice of contemplatives in the Zen and Christian traditions. We bow down together in awe, wonder, and gratitude to this great mystery.

6

Transcendent and Immanent

Essentially, to transcend means to go beyond. In the context of spirituality, transcendence means going beyond the material or physical world, to experience the transcendent. It means going beyond thoughts, concepts, and theories; beyond the limits of reason and linear logic; and beyond the conventional world alone. It means seeing beyond the sense of a separate self and any separation at all from the whole, from the one.

In Christianity, the transcendent is called God; in Zen, it is called emptiness, the absolute, the unborn, the unconditioned, or ultimate reality. Transcendence means going beyond thoughts, concepts, emotions, and images to experience that which is beyond anything we can conceive or imagine.

This transcendence informs our meditation practice. We let go of each thought that arises in the mind and come back to just breathing, just sitting, empty, open, aware. Letting go of thoughts, feelings, and images is a way to go beyond all that constricts and limits our experience of the transcendent that is always here. Yes, the transcendent is always here; we are the ones missing in action. The transcendent is hidden or covered over by our ceaseless thinking, worrying, plotting, and grasping after things and ideas. When we allow the bodymind to settle and open, when we are fully present, that which lies beyond appears.

In both Zen and Christianity, the transcendent is primary. It comes first and is eternity itself. This underscores the importance

31

of a daily contemplative practice like meditation or contemplative prayer. Without such a practice, the transcendent is likely to remain obscured by the busyness of life and by our incessant mental chatter.

In Zen, ultimate reality is beyond all words and concepts; therefore, we can say nothing about it. It is indescribable and thus beyond all attributes. In this sense, it is not typical in Zen to use the term *the transcendent* to describe ultimate reality.

The Christian tradition emphasizes that God is transcendent. God is more than, beyond, and independent of creation. Sometimes this emphasis makes people feel like God is beyond this world, residing far away in heaven, even though the Christian teaching is that God is everywhere including right here. God transcends time and space and is greater than the total of everything in the entire universe. God is beyond our human capacity to imagine or understand, but we can still engage in a personal relationship with God.

In the Zen and Christian traditions, God, or ultimate reality, is indescribable, inconceivable, and beyond the limits of human comprehension. God, or ultimate reality, transcends human nature and is not limited to a humanistic or scientific cause-and-effect worldview. Transcendence does not negate scientific or humanistic principles; it expands our horizons beyond them in a way that is enriching and transforming.

Often the concept of transcendence is contrasted with the concept of immanence. This sets up a dualistic approach to God or ultimate reality as being either transcendent or immanent. However, in Christianity the one God is considered both transcendent and immanent. The transcendent God is immanent in Jesus, in the Holy Spirit, and in each of us.

In emphasizing that ultimate reality is beyond all attributes, the great second-century Zen ancestor Nagarjuna would avoid saying that ultimate reality is transcendent, immanent, neither, or both. He warned us to avoid all extreme positions. We cannot say that ultimate reality is transcendent because it is also immanent.

We cannot say that it is immanent because it is empty and beyond all things. We cannot say anything about it, even that it exists or does not exist. It does not exist or cease to exist in the way things exist or cease to exist. Ultimate reality is not a thing (Siderits & Katsura 2013).

With that caution, I would say that Zen tends to emphasize the immanent and the nonseparation of the transcendent and immanent. This is seen in the nondual realization of *just this*. Ultimate reality is realized in the direct experience of what is right in front of you. Zen does not look for explanations for why things exist or happen the way they do. The point of Zen is to experience reality just as it is and respond appropriately and compassionately. *Just this* is not just a deep appreciation for the people and things around you. It is the simultaneous experience of the transcendent, immanent in every atom of everything and every person right here and now. The transcendent is not an abstraction; it is manifesting within and around you as *just this* with no separation whatsoever.

In Zen liturgy, we chant, "Buddha Nature pervades the whole universe, existing right here, now" (*Zen Peacemaker Order Service Book* 1997, 5). Buddha nature is another name for ultimate reality, which is beyond form, space, and time, and at the same time Buddha nature pervades the whole universe right here and now.

In recent years, some people have proposed an approach to Buddhism that is secular. However, Buddha nature does not simply refer to human nature. It points beyond the humanistic or secular to something more. In his review of the book *After Buddhism: Rethinking the Dharma for a Secular Age* by Stephen Batchelor (2015), Robert Kennedy suggests that a secular approach ignores the long Buddhist and Zen tradition of meditation through which one directly experiences the unconditioned, unborn, absolute, ultimate reality. Kennedy refers to a verse from *The Record of Transmitting the Light*: "The orphan light, marvelously vast, is never darkened" (Cook 2003, 92). Kennedy uses this poetic expression of the transcendent shining forth everywhere in the world to highlight the fact that rather than being a secular approach to human development and ethics, many people are drawn to Buddhism and Zen meditation as a path to direct intuitive insight into this orphan light "whose slightest touch is instantly recognized and can be life-changing" (Kennedy 2016, 37). While a secular approach to Buddhism may be helpful to many people, it truncates Buddhism and sells it short for those seeking spiritual transformation.

The third ancestor in the Zen lineage is Sanavasa. He studied with Ananda, who was Buddha's cousin. It is said that Ananda knew and could recite every teaching the Buddha ever gave. One day, Sanavasa asked his teacher, Ananda, "What kind of thing is the original unborn nature of all things?" (Cook 2003, 42). In response, Ananda reached over and tugged on Sanavasa's robe. With this gesture, Sanavasa was awakened.

The original unborn nature of all things refers to the transcendent. Ananda tugging on Sanavasa's robe is indicating that the transcendent is immanent. The transcendent and immanent are inseparable, close, and intimate. This has been the case all along, but we have to wake up to this great reality. You and everything around you are a manifestation of the original unborn nature of all things.

For me, Zen is a path of meditation that can be integrated with Christianity to expand my experience of God, in, as, and around me. A prayer I sometimes say before I sit down to meditate is as follows:

> Here I am Lord
> Empty
> Open
> Awake to perceive and receive you
> God is here.

God or ultimate reality is always here. When we show up with heart and mind open, we see it clearly.

7

Impersonal, Personal, and Beyond

Ultimate reality or God is not limited to being perceived as impersonal or as personal. Buddhism and Zen tend to emphasize the impersonal and use words such as *ultimate reality*, *the absolute*, and *thusness*. Sometimes Buddhism and Zen use the word *it* in order to avoid using personal pronouns such as *he* or *she*. Ultimate reality does not have qualities like things have qualities; ultimate reality is not a thing. It is indescribable, ineffable, and inconceivable. Ultimately, we can say nothing about it; we can't even say that it is impersonal or personal, or both, or neither. This helps us break out of a constricted, limited view of that which is beyond anything we can imagine.

The Christian view of God is often criticized for being too anthropomorphic and personal, and therefore too small and limited. Rather than God creating humans in God's image, the criticism is that humans have created God in their image. But the Judeo-Christian tradition warns against imagining that God is like human beings. In Psalm 50:21, God says, "You thought that I was one just like yourself. But now I rebuke you and lay the charge before you."

In the book of Job, God speaks to Job out of the whirlwind, challenging him to expand his vision of God beyond the merely human: "Were you there when I laid the foundation of the earth? . . . when the morning stars sang together and all the heavenly beings shouted for joy? . . . Do you know when the mountain goat gives birth? . . . Is it by your wisdom that the hawk soars, and spreads its wings toward the south?" (Job 38:4, 7; 39:26). Job concedes, saying, "I have uttered what I did not understand, things too wonderful for me, which I did not know" (Job 42:3). Although the imagery is personal, the message is that God is beyond our intellect, imagination, and understanding. Yet we can open to God or ultimate reality, and there is a tremendous awe and wonder in encountering the infinite who is beyond our human capacity to grasp intellectually or express in words.

Even though ultimate reality in Zen is usually presented in an impersonal way, personal language is used at times. In *Gateless Gate* a koan says, "Even Shakyamuni and Maitreya are servants of that one. Just tell me, who is that one?" (Yamada 1990, 212). This means that even the historical Buddha and the Buddha of the future are servants of that one, one who is greater yet. Mumon's commentary to this koan states, "If you clearly recognize that one, it will be just like meeting your father at the crossroads. It is not necessary to ask others whether it is he or not" (Yamada 1990, 212). This koan points toward the direct experience of one who is greater than you and worthy of your service. At the same time, you are not other than that one. When encountered, that one is instantly recognized and known intimately. This koan is not to be understood on an intellectual level, but rather through an intuitive leap by which you open to the direct experience of nonseparation or intimacy with that one.

Personal language is also used in the collection of Zen koans called *The Record of Transmitting the Light*. Ultimate reality is sometimes referred to as the Old Fellow, that One, or Him. For example, one verse says,

> That One whose whole life is extremely active and lively
> We call the One who raises his eyebrows and blinks. (Cook
>   2003, 187)

Everything you do is that One manifesting in the world in the form of you blinking, laughing, eating, running, or sitting still. In the world, you encounter that One manifesting in yourself and others and can relate in a loving and personal way.

A verse in the koan collection *The Book of Equanimity* says, "Donkey sees the well; well sees the donkey" (Wick 2005, 161). The donkey seeing the well is a metaphor for the spiritual seeker transcending the small self to experience ultimate reality. The well seeing the donkey takes it a step further to seeing yourself and the world through the eyes of ultimate reality. This experience is very personal and intimate. In seeing yourself and the world through the eyes of ultimate reality, great love and compassion arise toward yourself and all beings. This koan reminds me of Meister Eckhart's famous saying, "The eye in which I see God is the same eye in which God sees me. My eye and God's eye are one eye and one seeing, one knowing and one love" (McGinn 1986, 270).

Ken Wilber encourages breadth and balance in the way we experience and express ultimate reality (Wilber 2017a, 171–74). Based on his all-quadrants, all-levels integral model, he describes relating to ultimate reality or God in the first, second, and third persons. Relating to God or ultimate reality in the first person refers to the realization that I am a manifestation of God or ultimate reality. This allows the individual to transcend one's sense of a separate self and experience one's true identity as God or ultimate reality, realizing simultaneously that God or ultimate reality is greater than the sum of all individuals and all things. It is in this sense that Buddha, upon his enlightenment, spoke in terms of *I*, meaning his identity as ultimate reality, when he exclaimed, "I and the great earth and beings simultaneously achieve the Way" (Cook 2003, 29).

Now I skip ahead to describe the third-person view before coming back to discuss the second-person view. Experiencing God or ultimate reality in the third person is experiencing God or ultimate reality manifesting in the whole universe, in everything you encounter, as an interconnected, dynamic whole. This totality can be referred to using a third-person pronoun such as *it*.

Experiencing ultimate reality in the second person means experiencing ultimate reality as *you* or in Martin Buber's sense of *Thou*. This allows for a personal relationship or a sense of *we* with God, or ultimate reality. This does not mean you are falling back into duality since I and Thou are experienced as distinct but not separate. Sometimes these days, the personal or second-person aspect is downplayed among people practicing Eastern forms of meditation because it is considered too anthropomorphic, immature, or concrete. As part of a more complete and comprehensive spirituality, Wilber emphasizes the validity and value of relating to ultimate reality or God, not only in the first and third persons, but also in the second person as you or Thou:

> To realize that you can approach that Intelligence and directly resonate with it is a profound spiritual path. Further, a path of devotional surrender to this Intelligence (or simple awe and wonder at this infinite Mystery) gets at the egoic self-sense in a way that other approaches just can't: you can take up a 3rd-person view of Spirit as the Great Web of Life and still retain your ego; likewise, you can imagine a 1st-person view of Spirit as your own True Self, but that always allows the self in any form (including the small egoic self) to remain stuck in the picture somewhere. (Wilber 2017a, 173)

A personal relationship with ultimate reality or God is not something you outgrow with nondual awakening. The personal aspect can emerge anew or become even deeper with ongoing spiritual development. It expands the heart and helps keep the ego in its proper place, enabling you to function in the world, without the ego dominating or obscuring a greater reality. Wilber warns us that if you stick with just the first- and third-person experiences of ultimate reality or God, the ego can actually become inflated, and this can lead to significant problems for the individual and community.

There is a Zen koan in which Zen Master Tung-an asked his student, "What is really going on beneath this robe?" The master was referring to the patched robe worn by the Zen master. The student had no answer, so the master said, "To study and practice the Buddha way without reaching what is beneath the robe is the greatest pain. Now you ask me the question."

The student asked the master, "What is really going on beneath this robe?" The master answered, "Deep intimacy." With this the student was greatly awakened, and he bowed to the master in gratitude while crying so hard that tears soaked his robe. The master acknowledged the student's awakening and again asked him, "What is really going on beneath this robe?" The student said, "Deep intimacy." The master said, "And even deeper intimacy" (Hixon 1995, 199).

Deep intimacy is expressed in the well-known hymn "In the Garden" written by C. Austin Miles:

I come to the garden alone
While the dew is still on the roses.

Anyone who gets up early to meditate or pray at dawn before the noise and demands of the day begin knows the special quality of this time of day. The image of dew still on the roses conveys the softness, sweetness, and beauty of reaching out to a personal God who hears and responds. The refrain says,

And He walks with me, and he talks with me
And He tells me I am His own,
And the joy we share as we tarry there,
None other has ever known.

We each need some time alone with God through meditation and prayer in the garden, in the woods, or in a quiet corner of the home. This relationship is unique for each of us. It is a way to experience that you are loved and cherished. The love and joy experienced in this primary relationship will overflow into all your relationships and enrich all areas of your life.

There is a Zen story about this kind of companionship. The monks were preparing for a special service commemorating the anniversary of the death of their beloved teacher Masu. Amid their preparations, a monk named Nanquan asked, "Tomorrow we are going to provide offerings to Masu, but do you think that he will come?" Zen Master Dongshan replied, "If he has a companion, he will come" (Cook 2003, 194).

This story is about the fact that ultimate reality is always present, but we need to become aware of it. Entering into a relationship with ultimate reality is a way to become a companion. When we make ourselves available to be a companion, we will experience companionship, a second-person relationship with ultimate reality or God.

There is a Zen koan in *Gateless Gate* in which Zen Master Basho says to his disciples, "If you have a staff, I will give you a staff. If you have no staff, I will take it from you." In this koan, ultimate reality appears as a staff. In his commentary on this koan, Mumon says, "It helps me wade across a river when the bridge is down. It accompanies me to the village on a moonless night" (Sekida 2005, 125). Realization of ultimate reality is a help to us in troubled times and when the going gets rough. We all need this kind of support.

This is similar to the imagery in the Twenty-third Psalm. "Even though I walk through the darkest valley, I fear no evil; for you are with me; your rod and your staff—they comfort me" (Psalm 23:4).

Jesus speaks in terms of a personal relationship with ultimate reality or God when he tells his disciples, "I do not call you servants any longer, because the servant does not know what the master is doing; but I have called you friends, because I have made known to you everything that I have heard from my Father" (John 15:15). Jesus tells the disciples that even after his death,

"The Advocate, the Holy Spirit, whom the Father will send in my name, will teach you everything, and remind you of all that I have said to you" (John 14:26).

As human beings, we have a basic need for a companion, a friend, and an advocate. We can find this in each other and in ultimate reality or God by waking up to who we are, which is beyond our wildest imagination, and by being a companion, friend, and advocate.

8

Distinct but Not Separate

In the Zen tradition, there is an expression, "Not one, not two." This refers to the absolute and the relative. Absolute ultimate reality is sometimes called *empty oneness* or *the formless*. If we say the absolute and relative are one, we ignore the relative world where there are many different forms. It is also not correct to say that the absolute and the relative are two different things. First, the absolute is not a thing; it is empty and formless, without substance. Second, the absolute takes form and manifests as all the different forms in the relative world, so in this sense the forms are not separate from the absolute. Absolute and relative are not two. The relative world is a manifestation of the absolute. A third reason why it is more correct to say "not one, not two" is that we can say nothing at all about vast, inconceivable ultimate reality that is beyond words and concepts altogether. So, technically, according to Zen ancestor Nagarjuna, it is not even correct to say, "Not one, not two" (Siderits & Katsura 2013).

In addition, Zen also speaks in terms of three. We start out in life learning to function in the world of form. That is what many call the real world—the everyday world of work, family, friends, and play. Then we may become interested in ultimate reality and take up a spiritual practice such as Zen meditation to look deeply into this matter. Sitting in silence, we open ourselves to the direct experience of empty oneness. Gradually, and sometimes suddenly, an opening to ultimate reality may occur. This is called *kenshō*, awakening, or enlightenment. However, as we are warned in *The Identity of the Relative and Absolute*, "To encounter the absolute is not yet enlightenment" (*Zen Peacemaker Order Service Book 1997*, 7). We integrate this experience into life and see that the ordinary is extraordinary. Speaking metaphorically, we see the light of ultimate reality shining through all the forms we encounter including ourselves. We see and feel that we are one, and at the same time, utterly unique and precious. There is no separation whatsoever. This experience is called *nonduality*.

There is a Zen teaching that first there is a mountain, then there is no mountain, then there is a mountain. This is a simple way of expressing how three different experiences are actually one whole reality. At first, we experience the mountain as form. I live in the mountains of southwestern Virginia. People are drawn to this area because of the beauty of the mountains. They enjoy not only the inspiring view but also going out amid the trees and streams to hike the trails and climb the rocks. This is not just a physical experience but also a spiritual experience of being one with nature. It nurtures the spirit.

However, this experience doesn't necessarily lead to empty oneness, seeing beyond the separate self, beyond viewing the mountain as an object seen by a separate self as subject. The experience of empty oneness is what is meant by the phrase "then there is no mountain." In Buddhist terms, it is the experience of Buddha nature, the Buddha nature of yourself and everything around you. Zen Master Lex Hixon asserts that "Zen is not a religion of earthly nature but of Buddha nature, the Light that always shines. Yet what appears to us as Buddha nature is earthly nature as well. Cries out the living Buddha: They are not two!" (1995, 282).

When we come down from the mountaintop of experiencing inconceivable empty oneness and return to the world of form, we experience the mountain and everything else in a new way. We see empty oneness expressing itself in the form of mountains, rocks, flowing water, open skies, trees, animals, people, and everything we see. We experience one life with endless diversity. This is what is meant by "then there is a mountain again," but this time you are not separate from the mountain or from all of life. There is no veil in front of your eyes. In Zen, the experience of nonduality is called *just this*: the experience of life, just as it is, with no separation.

Zen distinguishes the experiences of form, formless, and *just this*, but ultimately, they are not three; they are one. For teaching purposes, one ultimate reality is divided into three in order to lead us to see clearly, appreciate, and live one whole and full life.

Christianity tends to use imagery and language that are more personal in its doctrine of the Trinity to convey three human experiences of one God. God the Father represents the utterly transcendent source of all creation, who is, at the same time, as close and loving as a father is to his child. Jesus, the son, is the incarnation of God, born on earth to dwell among us and teach us about God the Father, who is an inconceivable mystery. Jesus shows us by example how to live a life of love on this earth as sons and daughters of God. We are liberated by living a life of love. Jesus affirms that we, too, are manifestations of the great mystery that is God. The Holy Spirit is the presence of God in all of creation and an advocate we can see blowing in the wind and feel burning in our heart to empower us to live as Jesus taught us to live.

Rooted in the Jewish religion, Christianity has always joined in saying, "Hear, O Israel: the Lord our God, the Lord is one" (Mark 12:29). The doctrine of the Trinity is not meant to confuse people into thinking that somehow there are three Gods for Christians or that the Christian God is divided into three parts. Each is the one whole God. There has always been, is now, and always will be one God, one ultimate reality manifesting, and being experienced, interpreted, and expressed in many ways.

A Christian teaching dating back to the Council of Chalcedon in 451 confirms that Jesus's divinity and humanity are distinct but not separate realities united in one person who is one with God (Thompson 1994, 130). This principle of *distinct but not separate* applies not only to Jesus but also extends to all human beings as sons and daughters of God. *Distinct but not separate* has important implications with respect to the reality that we are already one and not separate from ultimate reality, or God. Yet we are distinct; we do not merge like a drop into the ocean—at this time, nor in the future.

There is a lovely image in the *Song of the Jewel Mirror Awareness* that poetically expresses being distinct but not separate from ultimate reality:

Filling a silver bowl with snow,
Hiding a heron in the moonlight.
When you array them, they are not the same;
When you mix them, you know where they are. (*Zen Peacemaker Order Service Book* 1997, 9)

Even though it is hard to make out the difference between the actual snow and the image of the snow, reflected in the shiny sides of a silver bowl, you can make out the difference. Similarly, you can discern the outline of a white heron standing still in the moonlight. The chant continues,

It is like facing a jewel mirror;
Form and image behold each other—
You are not it,
It is actually you. (*Zen Peacemaker Order Service Book* 1997, 9)

Even though I am a manifestation of God or ultimate reality, ultimate reality is infinitely greater than I or the total of all creation. At the same time, ultimate reality manifests in each person and creation in a distinct and particular way. We are one, distinct but not separate.

On the first day of winter I took the family dog, Roscoe, out into the backyard to play in the snow. Ordinarily, he likes to chase and retrieve tennis balls. Instead, I made snowballs and he chased them enthusiastically, but when he caught them in his mouth, they fell apart. He looked down to find them in the snow, but to no avail. He looked confused. Many people feel confused with all the talk in Zen and Christianity about one, two, and three. It is hard to grasp, because it does not follow our usual forms of logical, linear thinking. It is really not a matter of numbers at all. This is where meditation helps us take an intuitive leap into another way of knowing that is beyond words and numbers altogether.

9

Relationship, Identity, Intimacy

Growing up Christian, my faith and religious experiences were based on having a relationship with Jesus, and through Jesus with God. Walking hand in hand with Jesus allowed me to weather the inevitable ups and downs of life. Beyond that, it gave me a sense of what is most important and ultimate in life as a daughter of God. It was the bright spot in life and the hope of humanity and the earth. This sense of relationship with the ultimate highest reality is still the bedrock of my spirituality.

However, Zen showed me how to take another step, like an astronaut stepping out into space with nothing beneath her feet, only ultimate reality extending out in all directions. You leave the comfort of home, or your own little space capsule, and venture out into new territory. When we let go of all our thoughts about God or ultimate reality, and all our ideas about who we are in relationship to God and the world, we open to who we are at the deepest level, which is not separate from God or ultimate reality. We are as vast and spacious as the universe. You find your identity in God, who is greater than you and greater than you can ever imagine.

This shift from relationship to identity is mind-blowing and transformative. Christian teachings such as "You are Christ in this world" take on new meaning. This does not just mean that you are doing Christ's work by helping the poor, sick, and oppressed. You are not working alongside Christ; Christ takes form in you. You are a manifestation of the one God. You are ultimate reality

47

functioning in the world. You are Christ, right here and now. You are Buddha, awake and engaged. This does not do away with the human need for relationship with God, ultimate reality, or other people; nor is identity better than relationship. It does bring a powerful new dimension to life for which many people yearn.

Christianity includes teachings on identity, that we are one body, and that Christ lives in us. However, sitting in silent meditation helps you experience your oneness with Christ, and with others, as a living reality here and now, and not just as intellectual ideas in your head. When Roshi Kennedy distributes Communion, he often says, as did St. Augustine, "Receive what you are." This statement is always very moving to me and breathes new life into Christian teachings on identity.

The sutra called *The Identity of Relative and Absolute*, which is chanted in Zen services around the world, affirms that it is possible to experience your identity with ultimate reality. This is what Buddha awakened to under the Bodhi tree when he saw the morning star and exclaimed, "I and the great earth and beings simultaneously achieve the Way" (Cook 2003, 29). The *I* in Buddha's exclamation refers to ultimate reality and reflects Buddha's awakening to his own identity as inseparable from the great all-inclusive *I*. This is like the great I AM of the Jewish and Christian traditions. This awakening not only brings to life the realization of your true identity in ultimate reality but also the realization of your oneness with the great earth, all beings, and all the stars throughout the universe. It brings you into harmony with ultimate reality, the earth, the stars, and all beings as you walk the way together.

One evening, as my husband and I sat side by side on our cushions on the rug in the living room meditating together, as we often do, I heard the *ping, ping, ping* of raindrops hitting the skylights overhead. The sound of rain filled the room and washed over and through me. I was glad to be alive and hear like this. A Zen koan from *The Blue Cliff Record* called "Kyosei's Voice of Raindrops" came to life for me in that moment:

> Kyosei asked a monk, "What is the noise outside?" The monk said, "That is the voice of the raindrops." Kyosei said, "Men's thinking is topsy-turvy. Deluded by their own selves, they pursue things." (Sekida 2005, 273)

Kyosei's question is carefully crafted to elicit the monk's state of mind. The monk rises to the challenge and says, "It is the voice of the raindrops." He doesn't say, "It's raining outside." The monk's response shows that he has transcended the duality of inside and outside. Also, the monk does not objectify the rain. The monk does not experience himself as a subject hearing an object, the rain. He expresses that he is not separate from the raindrops and the hearing.

Kyosei follows up by saying that most people's thinking is topsy-turvy, meaning that they are deluded and lose themselves in pursuit of things. They objectify and view everything, including themselves, as mere things. This koan is calling us to transcend the duality of inside and outside and the duality of subject and object. Most of us are able to appreciate the sound of raindrops, but this koan urges us to take it a step further to experience hearing without a hearer, not only no object, but also no subject. First the object drops off and then the subject drops off and there is no separation at all, *just this ping, ping, ping*. This is not just oneness; it is also the particular sound we recognize as the voice of raindrops, which can be distinguished from all the other sounds of nature.

The first line of the verse to this koan says, "The empty hall resounds with the voice of raindrops" (Sekida 2005, 273). This is what Zen calls a *turning word*. It has the power to trigger a shift from relationship to identity. You are the empty hall when you sit silent and still in meditation, letting go of all thoughts, concepts, and images. Emptiness reverberates with the voice of raindrops. The empty hall is full of the voice of raindrops. Emptiness is fullness. The silence is the sound.

The experience of Buddha, and the experience of Zen practitioners and Zen masters down through the centuries, confirm that it is a human possibility to experience directly our identity in ultimate reality. Through meditation, you not only can experience nonduality or identity but also grow to be a truly intimate human being—intimate with God, or ultimate reality, intimate with yourself just as you are, intimate with others, and intimate with your life just as it is.

Intimacy is to know and be known. It is also being comfortable with not knowing and being open to something new and beyond your ability to anticipate or imagine. Intimacy is life itself, fresh and new, unfolding moment by moment. Intimacy is directly experiencing that you are not separate from ultimate reality or the whole of life. In Zen, this type of intimacy is sometimes called *just this*. It is like a veil has been lifted from in front of your face and nothing separates you and all that you see. Life is more vibrant and alive and real.

There is a farm about a mile from our house where you can go in June and July to pick blueberries, blackberries, and red raspberries. They send out an e-mail when the berries are ripe, and people from all over town descend on the fields like a flock of birds. Men, women, and children of all ages head out with buckets in hand to stand between the rows of berry bushes picking berries one by one. Since the farm is only about five miles from Virginia Tech, where there are students and faculty from around the world, you can hear chattering in English, Chinese, Spanish, German, Farsi, and various other languages floating through the air as you stand in the bright sun plucking berries directly from the bush and dropping them into your bucket. This is intimacy, *just this*, the juicy explosion of one ripe blueberry popped into your mouth on a summer day in the berry patch.

10

Boundless Love

The main teaching of Zen is identity—seeing through the illusion of a separate ego self to directly experience ultimate reality, which manifests as you, and the whole universe, from which you are not separate. When you see and feel that you are one with others, the earth, and all beings, love and compassion arise. You are moved to care for others and the earth as you would care for yourself and those closest to you.

The main teaching of Christianity is love—God's boundless love. "God is love, and those who abide in love abide in God, and God abides in them" (1 John 4:16). God's love is primary. "We love because he first loved us" (1 John 4:19). God loves us into existence, and this ongoing love permeates all creation. God has loved us since the beginning of time, loves us now, and will love us always. God's love is not bound by time or space. It is infinite, eternal, and boundless.

The first and most well-known koan in the *Mumonkan* is called Joshu's Mu. A monk asks Zen Master Joshu, "Does a dog have Buddha nature or not?" Joshu says, "Mu." In Japanese, Mu means "no." According to basic Buddhist teachings, everything is a manifestation of Buddha nature or empty oneness, so this reply does not make sense. Many Zen practitioners sit for years with this koan before penetrating and embodying its depths. The verse to this koan gives us a helpful pointer.

Dog—Buddha nature!
The perfect manifestation, the absolute command.
A little "has" or "has not,"
And body is lost! Life is lost! (Yamada 1990, 12)

It is not a matter of what you have or don't have, it is a matter of seeing clearly what and who you are beyond thoughts, words, and concepts. This insight is instantly life-giving, yet it is the work of a lifetime to embody it.

Applying this insight to the Christian teaching that "God is love" allows you to see that God's boundless love is not something you have or don't have. It is what you are. Nothing can separate you from the love of God, because it is what you are and what you have been created to embody and share with all humankind.

Psychologist Abraham Maslow, a founder of both humanistic and transpersonal psychology, is well known for developing a hierarchy of human needs (see Maslow 1970). He identified physiological needs, such as breathing, food, water, and elimination, as the most basic human needs that need to be met before a person can focus on meeting the next-higher level of needs, which are safety and security. The next level is the human need for love and belonging. It is essential to recognize our human need for love and belonging. Love is not optional. If we are not loved and do not belong to a family, a circle of friends, or a community where we can give and receive love, we do not thrive as infants, children, or adults.

Buddhists take refuge in the Buddha, the Dharma, and the sangha. The Buddha refers to awakening to Buddha nature, empty oneness, or ultimate reality, as Buddha did. The Dharma means the teaching or the particular truth of each person and thing, just as it is, as a manifestation of ultimate reality. The sangha is the community. Buddha emphasized the importance of contemplative practice in the context of community because this is where our insight is validated by those who have traveled the path before us. Sangha is where we learn to give and receive love as we walk the way together. Without love and tenderness, there is the danger of becoming stone Buddhas.

To be a follower of Jesus is to walk the path of love. Jesus said, "I give you a new commandment, that you love one another. Just as I have loved you, you also should love one another. By this everyone will know that you are my disciples if you have love for one another" (John 13:34–35). Sitting in silence in God's presence, presence sitting in presence, is a wonderful way to love the inconceivable God who is beyond words and concepts. But this is not enough, we must love God manifesting in this world. We must be God's boundless love in the world and love one another. When we love one another, we love God; we cannot separate loving God from loving the people in our life. We are one boundless love.

Roshi Janet Richardson has been a Zen and Christian teacher and role model for me. I was her attendant during the week of sesshin, an intensive Zen retreat, leading up to her dharma transmission ceremony, which is the ceremony that authorizes a person to be a Zen teacher. She told me that Roshi Kennedy wanted to give her a dharma name that meant Vehicle of Wisdom. She graciously told him that she preferred the name Jinne, which means Beloved of God. Of course, that is the name he gave her. Throughout her life as a Sister of St. Joseph of Peace, she reached out in love to people near at hand and around the world through her work at the United Nations and Catholic Relief Services. One day, she showed me the ring she received when she became a Catholic sister. Engraved inside are the words, "Love God Now." Now in her nineties, she still lives her life this way.

In my busy life as a wife, mother, nursing professor, and Zen teacher, it is essential to love myself as God loves me. When I treat myself with love, respect, compassion, and care, I am better able to embody God's love and share it with others. If we cannot accept the boundless love of God and experience our identity as a manifestation of God's love in the world, it constricts that ability to be warm, open, loving human beings. When we accept God's boundless love, we live with enthusiasm, loving life itself with all its joys and challenges.

When I was in nursing school, a classmate and I made a follow-up home visit to a young mother whose baby was born with multiple serious health problems, for which the best medicine of the time had no cure. The prognosis was that the baby would live for only a few months. We pulled up to the apartment building, which was in a run-down neighborhood in Dallas. We parked the car on the street and walked up the sidewalk to knock on the door. The young mother opened the door, happy to see us, and eager to learn all she could about providing the best care possible for her son. She proudly showed us her baby sleeping peacefully in a bassinette in what she explained was the warmest corner of the room. She was obviously a very conscientious mother, with all the baby's diapers, clothes, and supplies neatly stacked on top of the dresser. After we talked for a while, the baby woke up for his feeding. As she rocked, held, and talked to him, she seemed transfixed beholding the face of her infant son. Smiling and cooing with him she said to him several times, "You are my sweet baby boy. I love you so much." The love she had for her baby was palpable, and she was radiant in her love for him. It was as if she was giving the love of a lifetime to him and drinking in as much of his love and sweetness as she could during the short time they had together. This young mother did everything possible to comfort and take excellent care of her baby, and she lavished boundless love on him, a love that united mother and infant and allowed them to transcend the difficult realities they faced. This powerful lesson in love has lasted me a lifetime.

11

Incarnation

Although Easter is the height of the liturgical year, Christmas is the biggest holiday for most people growing up Christian in America. There is a special feeling to Christmas that draws people together to celebrate with family and friends. It's a time of warmth, lights, goodwill, and generosity.

We celebrate the incarnation of God—God taking human form in Jesus and being born on earth to live among us. This is not just true for Jesus; it is true for each of us, and it has been true for all time. God takes form and incarnates, or manifests, in each of us, and we have this marvelous opportunity to walk on the earth and look up at the stars.

Zen Master Bankei called ultimate reality the unborn (Waddell 2000). On Christmas, the unborn is born—amazing! Part of my job when I worked as a neonatal intensive care nurse was to be on standby in the delivery room during high-risk births. I was there to provide immediate care for the baby and transport him or her to the intensive care unit if needed. No matter how many births I attended, it was amazing every time new life came into the world. There is something special about a newborn. You can see, feel, and sense that they are fresh from heaven, fresh from the unborn to born.

The biggest holiday in the Zen world is Rohatsu. It commemorates the day of Buddha's enlightenment or awakening while meditating under the Bodhi tree. It is usually observed by a rigorous week of silent meditation that culminates on December 8 with a celebration meal. This too is a new birth, the birth of a new awareness. Although we are already a manifestation or incarnation of ultimate reality, we are born anew when we become aware of this reality. It is seeing for yourself that life is not just material, not just a matter of survival, not just suffering. We awaken and become aware of the unborn, the unmanifest, the highest reality that takes form when we are born into the world. It is awakening from distraction, from ignorance, and from the sense of a separate self. We awaken to the totality, to ultimate reality, to who we really are. This is a rebirth. We are called to be reborn and awaken moment by moment. This motivates us to keep sitting every day—awakening to the great reality functioning in ourselves and everything we see.

Zen speaks of the absolute and the relative, emptiness and form. These are not two separate things. The formless absolute takes form in the relative world. Another way to express this concept is to say that everyone embodies Buddha nature.

In Christian terms, God manifests in all creation. God is present in an ongoing way in creation. We are made in the image and likeness of God; God is present in us. This is what we celebrate on Christmas day. The transcendent God is born on earth as an infant. The light of God shines in the eyes of every infant. Birth is God and humanity, as one, saying yes to life.

The transcendent becomes immanent. Sometimes Jesus is called Emmanuel, which means "God with us." It is essential for us to realize that each of us is a manifestation of God and each of us is God with us. If you truly experience this, you treat yourself, your life, each other, the earth, and all beings with greater respect and love.

A phrase from the Hail Mary prayer says, "Holy Mary, Mother of God." This phrase goes deep for me because it is a feminine image of the holy or divine that elevates the usually low status of women. This is not true just for Mary; every woman who births or raises a child is a Mother of God. Every child is

God walking and playing and growing up on this good earth. Each child is Emmanuel, God with us. When we experience life in this way, we are joyful and inspired to be our best.

Incarnation means God or ultimate reality becomes flesh. We are not called to just think about the incarnation of God, or ultimate reality, but rather to realize and embody this great reality. Embodiment is an essential aspect of Zen practice. If we look at the typical Buddha statue, we see Buddha embodying his teaching. He calls us to sit down in meditation, let go of discursive thought, allow the body and mind to settle, and open to that which is beyond thoughts, emotions, and the sense of a separate self. Embodiment is not a discussion or theory. It's not speculation or abstract thought. It is a direct experience. Sit with every cell in your body awake and alert. Sit still and open. A verse at the end of *Gateless Gate* says,

> How does my hand compare with the Buddha's hand?
> Groping for the pillow at my back, I could feel it.
> In spite of myself I burst out laughing.
> From the first, the whole body is the hand. (Yamada 1990, 237)

The question "How does my hand compare with the Buddha's hand?" is not asking us to make comparisons. It is asking us to look and see for ourselves that our hand *is* Buddha's hand in the world. This is like a Christian seeing that his or her hands *are* Christ's hands in the world.

Incarnation or embodiment is not just an idea; it is a direct experience that can transform your life. The verse says, "I could feel it." This insight into ultimate reality manifesting in your hand, your whole body, and the whole world, from which you are not separate, is transformative and brings great joy. Sometimes it feels like you are finally getting the punch line of a joke and you erupt in joyful laughter.

The great reality incarnates and takes form in your very hands. Your hand contains not just your whole body but also the whole universe and beyond. In Zen, this is sometimes called *the one hand.*

Yamada Roshi says, "In the essential nature there is neither birth nor death" (Yamada 1990, 221). Ultimate reality, or God, is not born, nor does ultimate reality or God die. However, when ultimate reality or God takes form, there is birth and there is death. Each incarnation is unique and precious. It is through the particular that we learn about the transcendent and can embrace it.

My brother-in-law Reed died recently after living with diabetes since he was a child. He was married to my sister Lucy for forty years. He was a geophysicist who later became a high school science teacher in Dallas, where he had many Hispanic students. It was moving to hear how much he meant to his students over the years as a mentor, excellent science teacher, friend, and interesting human being. Many of his students attributed much of their success in life to having him as a teacher and to his many acts of kindness. We will not see Reed on this earth again, but his love for his wife, daughter, son, and students lives on. Many lives are better from knowing Reed as a particular incarnation born into the world. Each life is of great worth—our own life and the life of each person we influence and love.

My favorite Christmas carol is Placide Cappeau's "O Holy Night," and my favorite line from it is, "Till he appeared, and the soul felt its worth." Meditation is a way to sit silent and still and become ever more intimate with the unborn manifesting, appearing in the form of you and everyone around you. It is a way to take time to know, appreciate, and savor your own worth and the worth of those you love, the worth of every human being. Sitting silent and still you will see the unborn taking form before your very eyes on Christmas day and always. On Rohatsu and every day, we can awaken to the great reality taking form and being born moment by moment, fresh and new.

12

Radically Inclusive

Although we are always limited by the culture of our times, Buddha and Jesus both pushed the boundaries of their era with teachings that included people of different tribes, nations, religions, socioeconomic levels, and genders. For their times they were radically inclusive, and Buddhism and Christianity have continued to evolve—as various cultures around the world have evolved—toward being more and more inclusive. However, there is still a great need to continue to open our minds, hearts, and institutions to further growth in this direction.

Buddha stepped out of his inherited role in line to succeed his father as ruler of the Shakya tribe and became a wandering mendicant. He challenged the caste system and the role of the Brahmins as the sole religious leaders to whom the people were beholden to do rituals in order to gain favors from the gods. It was a radical and contested move on Buddha's part, to admit women to his sangha, albeit in a lesser and limited role. Although he was reluctant at first, he acquiesced to the pleading of his aunt, Mahaprajapati. He asserted that all human beings have the capacity to awaken to ultimate reality in this lifetime, regardless of caste or gender.

While Jesus did not set out to start a new religion, his following expanded to include Gentiles as well as Jewish people. He broke with the norms of his time by eating with tax collectors, prostitutes, the sick, and the poor. He was a healer and advocate for the oppressed and marginalized people in society. Drinking water given to him by a Samaritan woman was an example of how he transcended tribal and gender boundaries. His teachings to not judge others and to love your enemies were radically inclusive.

Zen practice opens us to the direct experience of unbounded awareness. When we sit down to meditate, we let go of all thoughts, words, and concepts that divide reality into parts. We open to the totality, the undivided wholeness of life. Unmanifest ultimate reality is boundless and includes everything. You are not separate from ultimate reality as it manifests in everything you see. Nothing is excluded.

There is a well-known Zen koan in which the monk asks Zen Master Unmon, "What is Buddha?" Unmon replies, "A dried shit-stick!" (Yamada 1990, 102). This is referring to a stick that was used at the time instead of toilet paper. The point of this koan is not to denigrate Buddha or to be cool and irreverent. It is making the serious point that everything is a manifestation of ultimate reality. Ultimate reality transcends the duality between holy and unholy, pure and impure. Nothing is excluded.

This insight into reality is fundamental as we face difficult circumstances in life. As a nurse I take care of people experiencing all kinds of physical and mental illnesses. When a patient vomits or has diarrhea, I am there to help the patient and clean up. This is part of life, and I am called to respond with compassion. A police officer who is the first responder to a freeway accident shows up to help, even amid blood, injury, broken glass, and danger from spilled fuel.

This is like the parable Jesus tells of the Good Samaritan. A man on the road to Jerusalem was beaten, robbed, and left half dead in the ditch beside the road. First a priest came by and crossed over to the other side of the road without helping the injured man. Then a Levite passed him by. Finally, a Samaritan came and helped the man by binding his wounds and taking him down the road to an inn where he paid the innkeeper to continue caring for the man. Jesus goes beyond cultural barriers when he makes the Samaritan the hero in this story despite the enmity between Samaritans and

Jews. Jesus tells this story in response to the question "Who is my neighbor?" (Luke 10:29). It expands our hearts to see that anyone we meet on the road is our neighbor; no one is a stranger. We should not look the other way or pass by the needs of people because they are in a group different from our own.

Three tenets of the Zen Peacemaker Order, established by Roshi Bernie Glassman, are not knowing, bearing witness, and loving action. Not knowing invites us to let go of fixed ideas about ourselves, others, and the world. Bearing witness allows us to listen, see, and have empathy for the joys and sufferings of others. Loving action encourages us to engage in compassionate action appropriate to the situation. Part of bearing witness is to not look away from the difficult aspects of life, but to be fully present to all of life.

Zen has a long history—extending back to National Teacher Chu Kokushi, who lived in the eighth century in ancient China—of drawing circles called *enso* to express Zen insight. These circles carry us beyond words and logic. They are spontaneous expressions of ultimate reality, the universe, or infinity. The enso includes everything, the whole. It is a symbol of radical inclusivity. Everything is included throughout space and time. In its emptiness the circle contains everything that ever was, is, or will be. The circle is a symbol of the fullness of life, round and complete like the sun, the moon, and the turning of the seasons.

In a book edited by Audrey Yoshiko Seo, I saw an enso with words written under it that said, "Please eat this" (2007, 75). This reminds me of the koan in which a monk asks Zen Master Ummon, "What is the teaching that transcends the Buddha and patriarchs?" Ummon says, "A sesame bun" (Sekida 2005, 349). Everything—even the most everyday object like a rice cake, a cookie, or a sesame bun—is a manifestation of ultimate reality.

While this is an ancient Zen idea, it is a new interpretation in Christianity. Theologian Elizabeth Johnson calls this insight *deep incarnation*. Johnson proposes that when the Gospel of John says that the Word of God became flesh, it refers not only to Jesus Christ but also to all human beings and that "it also reaches beyond us to join the whole evolving biological world of living creatures and the cosmic dust of which they are composed" (2018, 186). God is present in all creation, but also transcends creation. To be inclusive, we need to be open to new ideas and integrate them into our traditions, which have evolved and continue to evolve as new knowledge comes to light.

Jesus told his disciples, "Go into all the world and proclaim the good news to the whole creation" (Mark 16:15). He did not say go out and conquer the whole world and force people everywhere to believe as you believe. Religion should not divide us into boxes and generate conflict; rather, religion should open us to the one God, the one ultimate reality, as one people living in harmony with the earth and all its creatures.

There is a wonderful biography of Nicholas Black Elk, who is best known as a Lakota Sioux medicine man. Less well known is that, for decades in his later years, he was a Catholic catechist. He is now under consideration for sainthood in the Catholic Church. Many Native Americans were open to the teachings of Christianity and wanted to add these new teachings to their traditional religious beliefs and practices. Today, we call this *interspiritual practice*. Nicholas Black Elk was a pioneer in the field of interspirituality and is a role model for how to do it.

Tragically, many Christian missionaries forced people to forsake their native culture and religion, demanding that they practice Christianity exclusively. Christianity does not need to be an exclusive religion. Reverend Murray Rogers, an Anglican priest who served as a missionary in India for many years, emphasized that people should not be forced to choose (2006). They can be enriched and enlivened by more than one religious tradition. Religious traditions evolve, and as they do, hopefully they learn from mistakes made in the past and grow in appreciation for both their oneness and differences. Interspiritual practice creates bridges between religious traditions that help transform divisiveness into inclusivity, mutual enrichment, and warm welcome.

13

Suffering and Crucifixion

Buddha's Four Noble Truths are aimed at acknowledging and alleviating suffering. The First Noble Truth is that there is suffering in life, such as the discomfort, pain, and loss that come with old age, disease, and death. The Second Noble Truth identifies the cause of suffering, which is selfish clinging. The Third Noble Truth says that the end of suffering can be found in letting go of selfish clinging. The Fourth Noble Truth describes a way to do this by following the Eightfold Path. The strength of Buddha's teaching is that—by example and through the Eightfold Path he lays before us—he shows us how to meditate and free the mind from the bonds we place upon it.

During meditation, we let go of thoughts and bring our attention back to an awareness of the belly rising and receding as we breathe naturally. Or we can come back to an awareness of just sitting in the upright posture of meditation. We don't intentionally engage in thinking or problem solving or storytelling during meditation. Often, we notice the same types of thoughts arising in the mind repeatedly, which gives us insight into the way the mind works and issues that concern us. The process of continuously letting go of thoughts and bringing the attention back to the breathing, or just sitting with open awareness, tends to loosen the grip of our thoughts on us. We see that thoughts come and go. We see that emotions come and go. As we become less identified with our thoughts and emotions, we see that we are more than our thoughts and emotions. We gain a broader perspective and spaciousness in life. We have room to breathe and space to heal.

We see that clinging to thoughts and expectations about how we want our life to be, rather than how it actually is, creates discontent. Various forms of cognitive therapy help people develop more helpful and realistic thoughts. Newer forms of cognitive therapy incorporate mindfulness to help people not only change the content of their thoughts but also become aware of the way that thoughts and emotions arise and dissipate. People become less identified with and limited by their thoughts and emotions, which come and go. This application of Buddha's teachings has been effective in decreasing selfish clinging and alleviating the suffering of many people with depression and anxiety.

Insight into selfish clinging and the way it aggravates mental, physical, and relationship problems can significantly reduce human suffering, but many types of suffering remain to be endured. Around the world, people face war, violence, natural disasters, accidents, poverty, major mental illnesses like schizophrenia and dementia, and serious physical illnesses. As long as we have a body, we are faced with the possibility of pain and disability.

As I was writing this chapter, I learned that my fifteen-year-old granddaughter, Elise, needed to have hip surgery a second time and was scheduled for surgery in three weeks. She injured her hip playing soccer and had surgery to repair her hip five months ago. The recovery process involved no weight-bearing on the injured side, wearing support hose, and sleeping eight hours each night with her leg in a machine that moved her leg slowly back and forth. The initial recovery phase was followed by weeks of using crutches and going to several physical therapy sessions each week. It was a long and painful process, and she missed a month of her first year of high school.

The pain and suffering of hip surgery were put in perspective for her when she spent the night in the children's hospital after her surgery. In an adjoining room was a teenage girl with cancer.

Elise was awakened during the night by the girl crying in pain and begging her parents and nurse not to allow anyone to hurt her anymore by drawing blood. Elise had great empathy for the girl. She was grateful that she did not have cancer and that she only had to spend one night in the hospital.

However, even though Elise was grateful and had a good attitude, she was very upset that her hip did not heal properly, and that she would have to go through the whole difficult process again. It's hard to face repeating the pain, nausea, immobility, and missed school. She knew her parents, family, and friends would be there for her to do all they can to alleviate her suffering. They would suffer too, as they accompany her through the experience a second time.

As a nurse working in the neonatal intensive care unit, it was incredibly sad to see a tiny baby get a rough start in life and to watch the parents suffer hour by hour through the ordeal. We did everything we could to keep the babies comfortable, placing them in warming beds, positioning them on sheepskin, and doing procedures as gently as possible. However, one father told me that having his daughter in the neonatal intensive care unit was excruciating for him. He said it was like watching her be crucified.

Whenever innocent people suffer, I think of the slaughter of the innocents, which happened not only two thousand years ago in Bethlehem but many times, in many ways, around the world down to this day. In times of suffering, especially of the innocent, we ask why. There is no answer to this question on the level of thoughts and words. God or ultimate reality is inconceivable, and so is suffering. All we can do is allow it to break our heart open and call forth great love, kindness, and compassionate action from the depths of our soul.

Most Christians believe that Jesus died on the cross to save us from our sins. He was innocent, but he made the ultimate sacrifice to redeem his people. Some Christians believe that Jesus saved us by his loving example of how to live according to God's values, rather than by his suffering and death.

My Zen teacher, Roshi Kennedy, once told us that a pivotal Zen story for him was about a Zen teacher who took a walk into the mountains and came upon a shrine where priests were sacrificing oxen to gain some favor from the gods. The Zen teacher turned over the altar and liberated the oxen. The story reminded him of an experience he had when he was on a trip in Kathmandu. He took a walk into the hills and came upon a temple where priests were sacrificing goats and chickens. Blood was running down the hillside. He slipped in the blood and nearly fell. He thought, *Wow, I'm experiencing that Zen story right here, now!* Not only did he want to liberate the animals but also the animal or unconscious side of us as human beings, to expand our awareness of these aspects of ourselves, and allow us to integrate them appropriately, thereby freeing us to live full, whole lives.

This story is like God, who in the vision of Isaiah says, "What to me is the multitude of your sacrifices . . . I do not delight in the blood of bulls, or of lambs, or of goats" (1:11). Instead, what is pleasing in the eyes of God is that his people "cease to do evil, learn to do good; seek justice, rescue the oppressed, defend the orphan, plead for the widow" (Isa. 1:17). This liberates us to accept new interpretations of Jesus's death on the cross and integrate them with traditional interpretations.

Theologian Roger Haight (2016) suggests that an alternative interpretation of the crucifixion is that Jesus was crucified because his teachings threatened Roman rule in Jerusalem. Jesus taught that God is a loving God, and he stood up for people who were oppressed or marginalized. This threatened the status quo, and the people in power feared that Jesus's teachings would cause insurrection. Jesus lived an unselfish life and taught God's values, which ran counter to society's values at the time. Jesus stood up for God's values and was not willing to back down, even though it led to his crucifixion.

The cross takes on new meaning when viewed as Jesus suffering because he stood up for the people to bring them justice and liberation. Jesus—as a manifestation of God, hanging on the cross—shows that God suffers. Whenever his people suffer, God suffers.

We too are manifestations of God, and when we suffer, God knows our suffering and tears, and God is present. At times, we may feel that God has abandoned us, and in those times, we may call out like Jesus did on the cross, "My God, my God, why have you forsaken me?" (Mark 15:34). Jesus was human. It is okay to be fully human and express pain, fear, and loneliness. However, on a deeper level, we know as manifestations of God or ultimate reality that we do not suffer alone. We know that God suffers with us, and as us, and that we suffer in solidarity with all who have suffered in the past, who suffer now, or will suffer in the future. We are not separate from God or ultimate reality.

Buddha sitting in meditation and Jesus hanging on the cross both provide ways to alleviate the suffering that comes from viewing yourself as a limited, separate self. They help you experience self-transcendence by recognizing your true identity as a manifestation of God or ultimate reality. In recognizing this, you experience unity with all creation. You do not suffer alone. This realization brings comfort and courage in difficult or terrible times. You see that you are greater than whatever pain or adversity you encounter. In troubled times, you are called to be loving and compassionate toward yourself and others. In this way, your heart expands. You learn to surrender into the arms of a greater reality, the one God, the one ultimate reality, and there you find strength, power, rest, and boundless love.

14

Death and Resurrection

The death and resurrection of Jesus Christ are central to Christianity, so it is important to plumb the depths of their significance. The story of the resurrection is told differently in the various books of the New Testament, leaving this event open to interpretation. Sitting silently in meditation during Lent and throughout the year has opened my mind and heart to new insights regarding this great mystery. The resurrection can be experienced on many levels, and all of them are powerful and transformative.

For many years, New River Zen Community held our weekly group meditation sessions in the nursery of a church. During Holy Week, the parishioners filled the room with plants to re-create the Garden of Gethsemane. On Good Friday, members of the Zen group, along with parishioners, took turns sitting in silent vigil throughout the night. Sitting in silence together at this holiest time of the year was a deeply meaningful expression of interfaith practice.

In the mid-1990s, Charles and I traveled with Roshi Kennedy to LaSalle Haus, a Jesuit Retreat Center near Zug, Switzerland, to attend an interfaith conference convened by Roshi Niklaus Brantchen. Zen Master and Professor Ryomin Akizuki traveled from his home in Japan to present a paper at the conference, but shortly after arriving in Switzerland he had a stroke and was unable to present the paper, so I never had the opportunity to meet him. Fortunately, he distributed a copy of his paper, which discusses the common ground of Buddhism and Christianity. His insightful ideas on this topic were informed by his work as a religious scholar, his training and practice as a Zen master, and his baptism as a Protestant in his youth. He says, "As a Zen Buddhist, or rather as a man of religion, I have learned some profound lessons from Christianity." He goes on to say, "Though I am a Buddhist, I believe that the ultimate in religion is represented by the phrase 'Immanuel (God with us)' in the Bible" (Akizuki 1994, 5). He contends that common ground between Buddhism and Christianity lies in the experience of Immanuel, or God with us. In both religions, we realize that God or ultimate reality is manifested in us when we become egoless. The Buddhist lets go of the separate ego and experiences empty oneness (*shunyata*), or oneness with ultimate reality. The Christian dies to his or her ego and is resurrected to new life, as one with God, through the death and resurrection of Christ.

When we speak of death, it can mean not only the body's physical death but also death of the ego or the sense of a separate self, death to selfish clinging, and death to behavior motivated by selfishness. Resurrection, as life after death, not only means life after the death of the physical body but also new life that comes with insight into our oneness with ultimate reality or God and all creation.

In Zen, form and emptiness are both transcended in awakening to the nondual experience of *just this*. There is no separate self as an observer of life, and there is no thing or object being observed; life is a dynamic manifestation of ultimate reality standing, sitting, running, cooking, eating, cleaning, laughing, crying, birthing, and dying. When we awaken to *just this*, we see that life is larger than death.

Jesus prayed to God for his disciples, saying, "This is eternal life, that they may know you, the only true God, and Jesus Christ whom you have sent" (John 17:3). We do not need to wait until after death to experience eternal life. We can transcend the bonds of time and space and experience our oneness with God right here and now. We can transcend our sense of separation from God and others by letting go of the ego, selfish clinging, and selfish behavior right now, and experience love alive in us, others, and the world. The risen Christ, Immanuel, God with us, is alive right here and now.

From the Zen perspective, eternal life does not mean endless time, but rather the transcending of time altogether. We awaken each moment to eternal, unbounded ultimate reality. Unbounded means undivided. The totality of life is not divided into hours, minutes, and seconds, nor into past, present, and future. Therefore, the question of what happens to us after death loses its meaning in the experience that there is no before and after. The experience of undivided oneness is vast and eternal.

In a wonderful scene in Leo Tolstoy's *Resurrection*, on Easter morning in front of the church, parishioners are exchanging hugs, kisses, and Easter greetings. One of the parishioners says to another that Christ is risen, her tone implying that on this day we are all equal (Tolstoy 1899, 62). It has become a family tradition that my husband and I joyously say to each other each year on Easter morning, "Christ is risen! Today all are equal!" This expression proclaims the equality of all people and the way we should love and treat one another, regardless of social status, income level, race, or gender. Equality does not mean that we are all the same, or that we are the same as God, but rather that we are one with God and each other. It is indeed a resurrection to new life when we wake up to this reality and embody it in life to the best of our ability.

Zen meditation is a way to let go of ego, by letting go of thoughts, images, and opinions, and returning attention to the breath, or posture, as we sit in the present, awake and alert. When we do this, we become aware of that which is larger than our small, separate ego. We open to something larger than our preconceived notions. Zazen is moment by moment death and resurrection. It is death to the separate ego-dominated self and rebirth to our fundamental oneness in ultimate reality or God, oneness with the totality. Death and resurrection do not take place by thinking or reading about them. Transformation does not take place on an intellectual level. It takes place by not being distracted, fragmented, or preoccupied. It is experienced in being fully present to life itself. It is in breathing, hearing, seeing, tasting, feeling, and living fully without separation. The whole unity breathes, hears, sees, tastes, feels, and is alive.

Theologian Roger Haight writes, "In the end, confidence in resurrection makes the cross meaningful by negating its ultimacy" (2016, 56). Evil, pain, and suffering in life are only part of a greater reality, and in that sense they are not ultimate. We cannot minimize them or explain them away. We must acknowledge that they are part of life as a human being and thus a manifestation of inconceivable ultimate reality or the mystery that is God.

In our limitations as human beings we do not have the capacity to understand this fully. Paul speaks eloquently about the ultimacy of love. He also speaks of not knowing, saying, "For we know only in part, and we prophesy only in part; but when the complete comes, the partial will come to an end. . . . For now we see in a mirror dimly, but then we will see face-to-face. Now I know only in part; then I will know fully, even as I have been fully known" (1 Cor. 13:9–12).

Ultimately, Christians are confident that, in life and in death, they are fully known and fully loved by the infinite God. Christians share with Zen masters and practitioners a sense of oneness with God or ultimate reality, and a deep acknowledgment and embrace of not knowing.

15

Grace and Gift

Grace is the presence of God in your life. It is infinite and pervades the whole universe. It is already here, but you need to become aware of it, open your heart to it, accept it, be embraced by it, and allow it to influence the way you live.

Sitting in silent meditation, open, aware, and fully present, is a way to experience presence—your own presence and God's presence—which are ultimately one. Zazen is a way to experience the infinite subtlety of ultimate reality, or God. In the silence and stillness of meditation, this subtle reality can come into the foreground of your attention.

A verse in *Gateless Gate* reads,

Just because it is so clear,
It takes us longer to realize it.
If you quickly acknowledge that the candlelight is fire,
You will find that the rice has long been cooked. (Yamada
     1990, 40)

Ultimate reality or God is present everywhere, within and around us. However, we are so busy and distracted that it may take us a long time to realize it and for this insight to transform the way we live. A contemplative practice such as silent, wordless meditation is helpful here. Being fully present and transcending the separate self reveal experientially that our presence is to God's presence as candlelight is to fire. When we see this clearly, we can acknowledge that this has always been the case. Sometimes it takes us a long while to wake up and come home to this liberating and joyous reality.

Grace is a gift that is freely given to everyone. It cannot be earned. This teaching is present in many branches of Christianity and in Zen. In the Zen tradition, Bodhidharma is credited with traveling from India to China in the sixth century to introduce Zen to the people there. There is a well-known story about the first meeting between Bodhidharma and Emperor Wu who was an early patron and practitioner of Buddhism in China. Emperor Wu told Bodhidharma about all the monasteries he had built, all the scriptures he had translated, and all the monks he supported, and he asked Bodhidharma, "What merit will I get from all this?" Bodhidharma replied, "There is no merit" (Cleary & Cleary 2005, 3). In other words, you cannot earn favor or enlightenment; you cannot buy your way into heaven. Ultimate reality is already present. It is not a thing, not a commodity. It cannot be bought and sold. It is freely given. Wake up and see this for yourself and be it for others.

No *merit* is a hard concept to comprehend. We are prone to judge some people more worthy of divine grace, favor, and presence than others. This tendency is highlighted in two parables that Jesus told. In the parable of the Laborers in the Vineyard, a landowner hired laborers who went to work in his vineyard first thing in the morning. Several times during the day, he hired additional laborers who began their work in the vineyard much later than the first group. At the end of the workday, he paid first those who were hired last, and paid all the laborers the same amount regardless of how many hours they worked. The laborers hired earlier in the day complained, even though they received their agreed-upon full day's wages (see Matt. 20:1–16). This story makes the point that God's grace or favor is not quantifiable. It is not a numbers game. It is not earned; it is freely given. God's generosity extends to all. The human tendency to compare yourself to others and to be envious if someone seems to be getting a better deal in life than you fuels discontent, conflict, and suffering.

There is a similar theme in the parable of the Prodigal Son and his brother. The older brother conscientiously worked on the family land for years, while his younger sibling went off and squandered his inheritance on dissolute living. When the younger brother finally came home, poor and destitute, the father welcomed him with open arms and had a feast in his honor. When the older brother came in from the fields and heard the party going on, he was angry with his father and refused to join the celebration. He complained to his father that it wasn't fair, because he was obedient and hardworking for years, and the father never had a feast in his honor. The father replied, "Son, you are always with me, and all that is mine is yours. But we had to celebrate and rejoice, because this brother of yours was dead and has come to life; he was lost and has been found" (Luke 15:31–32).

Many if not all of us can identify with the human emotions expressed by the older brother when we have faced situations at home or at work where we felt we did more than our share of the work, while others goofed off. Sometimes we feel frustrated, discouraged, or angry; we feel that we are not acknowledged or rewarded sufficiently for our efforts. We need to stand up for ourselves in such situations, yet we also need to see that comparisons with others, envy, discontent with perceived inequalities, and refusal to share in the joy of others add to our own suffering. The father in the parable models the joy that comes with forgiveness and generosity extended to all, especially to those most in need.

The father's statement, "All that is mine is yours," is an expression of pure gift, pure grace. Life itself is a gift. It is a gift to wake up each morning and greet the new day. We are gifted with family and friends. Most of us in this country have food to eat and enough to share. We have clean water to bathe in and drink. With the changing seasons come snow in winter; daffodils, tulips, and forsythia in spring; green grass and swimming in summer;

and leaves of red, yellow, and flaming orange in fall. "From his fullness we have all received, grace upon grace" (John 1:16).

Some people break open in life's darkest hour amid addiction, disaster, illness, or loss, and they have a deep, life-changing experience of grace. However, I know from many years working in the field of psychiatric nursing that, unfortunately, many people do not experience God's presence at such times. Their suffering continues, and some are so overwhelmed that they resort to suicide—another part of the inconceivable mystery of ultimate reality, God, and life.

In his book *Getting Life*, Michael Morton (2014) tells about his experience of the presence of God amid the extreme suffering of serving a life sentence in a prison in Texas where he was convicted of murdering his wife, a crime he did not commit. Fourteen years into his time in prison, during one of his darkest hours when he found out that his son was changing his name and being officially adopted, he hit rock bottom. He cried out to God, but day after day went on with no response. Then one ordinary evening when he went to bed, suddenly he was bathed in God's light, peace, joy, and love. During the following months through his continuous contemplation, reading, conversation, and prayer, he came to know three simple but profound truths about God: "he exists, he is wise beyond any human calculation, and he loves me" (Morton n.d.). This brought peace and new meaning to his life during the remaining eleven years he spent in prison prior to his exoneration based on DNA evidence.

Jesus told Nicodemus, "The wind blows where it chooses, and you can hear the sound of it, but you do not know where it comes from or where it goes. So it is with everyone who is born of the Spirit" (John 3:8). It is grace or gift that you have an interest in meditation, God, or ultimate reality, and that leads you to pick up this book and learn more. As we grow and develop, our ideas about God, ultimate reality, and spirituality may change and evolve. Sometimes our old certainty must give way for new possibilities to emerge. This may feel like a loss, but in time we see that the loss of our old ideas is necessary to open to a fuller experience of ultimate reality or God. What at first felt like a loss turns out to be a blessing.

We can invite, but we cannot force spiritual growth or insight. It is a gift that comes in its own good time. In Zen, we sit in meditation like Buddha did, with trust in his insight, and open to the possibility that we too can realize our oneness with ultimate reality. At the same time, we sit without grasping after anything, without any sense of lack, without desire for attainment. We sit with energy and attention, but not with the tension of striving or trying to achieve something. Insight is not an achievement. There is nothing that we lack, nothing to be attained. We are already one with ultimate reality; we simply sit in its presence. It is already present, already given. Insight is pure grace, pure gift. Everything is gift.

Part III

Discovering the Nonseparate Self

16

Who Am I?

Basic spiritual questions people have asked down through the ages are "Who am I?" "How did I get here?" "What am I here for?" and "Where am I going after I die?" When we sit down to do Zen meditation, we don't think about these questions, but we are hoping that Zen practice sheds light on these ultimate concerns for us.

When Charles and I lived on the Navajo reservation, the Navajo people knew where they came from as told in their creation story, and they knew who they were as members of their tribe and as members of their mother's clan and their father's clan. Each of the different Native American tribes has its own creation story and kinship patterns, giving members a sense of who they are and where they came from as individuals and as a tribe.

Today, most of us in the United States don't have a tribe. We grew up in a predominantly Judeo-Christian culture and learned the creation story of Adam and Eve from Genesis. We also studied Charles Darwin and the evolution of life on this planet, including the evolution of Homo sapiens. We have a scientific answer to our question about how we got here, and we have a religious answer that tells us that God created us. If we do not interpret the Adam and Eve story literally, we can hold both stories as meaningful answers to the question of how we got here.

Zen focuses on the question "Who am I?" The question is not answered verbally but through the direct experience of *shunyata* or emptiness. The intuitive experience of emptiness catapults us beyond the experience of a separate self. Your eyes are opened to the reality that you are not a separate thing; you are not a thing at all. All phenomena, including yourself, are empty, and in this emptiness, all are one. There is no separate subject observing separate objects. There is *just this* nondual experience of emptiness manifesting in life itself—walking, singing, splashing, drinking, and chopping bright orange carrots, *chop, chop, chop, chop*. In Zen terms, this is called *awakening*.

The Zen koan "Show me your original face before your mother and father were born" elicits a direct experience of emptiness and insight into "Who am I?" as a manifestation of emptiness. Rather than a creation story, this koan provides a different way to see deeply into the question "How did I get here?" This insight transcends space and time. It helps you see beyond your biological family, beyond genetics, beyond tribe and clan and culture altogether, to experience ultimate reality manifesting in the world in who you are right here and now. At the same time, it does not negate family, biology, or cultural aspects of our particular life in the world. The universal and particular are both fully appreciated.

The Zen sutra *Identity of Relative and Absolute* says, "To encounter the Absolute is not yet enlightenment" (*Zen Peacemaker Order Service Book* 1997, 7). The absolute manifests as all the different phenomena in the relative world. Each person is a unique manifestation of the absolute or ultimate reality. The direct experience of emptiness allows you to see the underlying unity of yourself, other people, animals, trees, rivers, and mountains. To experience this underlying unity and to live your life with the love, respect, and reverence that it engenders are what is meant by enlightenment. To do this in each situation you encounter is why you are here.

Another answer to the question "What am I here for?" is found in the verse chanted each evening in many Zen centers:

Let me respectfully remind you
Life and death are of supreme importance

Time swiftly passes by and opportunity is lost
Each of us must strive to awaken. . . .
Awaken. . . .
Take heed.
This night your days are diminished by one.
Do not squander your life. (Still Mind Zendo n.d.)

We are here to awaken. This verse reminds us of our mortality as human beings and that our time on this earth is short.

In the nondual awakening of Zen, space and time are transcended so there is no coming or going, no here or there, and no division of time into past, present, and future. Therefore, the question "Where am I going after I die?" is not answered with a verbal explanation, but in the ineffable direct experience of emptiness that transcends before and after. We are urged to awaken to ultimate reality right now. Don't wait until after you die.

There are many different schools of Buddhism, some of which teach the doctrine of *anatman* or "no-self." Ken Wilber notes that beginning with the Indian Buddhist philosopher Nagarjuna in the second century, the Mahayana and Vajrayana schools began to teach that "absolute reality (Emptiness) is radically Nondual (adraya)—in itself it is neither self nor no-self, neither atman nor anatman, neither permanent nor momentary/flux" (1995, 693). The absolute, or ultimate reality, transcends all concepts and can only be realized through direct nondual experience. Sitting in silent wordless meditation, beyond all thoughts and categories, provides the opportunity for your awareness to become clear and open to the nondual experience of form as an expression of emptiness that Zen calls *thusness* or *suchness*.

Wilber contends that the concept of no-self is not accurate or helpful in understanding either the relative or the absolute. "Both the cohesive self and the momentary states are relatively real, but both are ultimately Empty" (Wilber 1995, 695). The momentary states are what Buddhists call the five *skandhas*: form, sensation, perception, mental activities, and consciousness. We can say nothing about inconceivable absolute reality. It has no qualities; thus, we cannot describe it as the realm where no-self is the ultimate truth. Rather than saying that there is no self, it is more accurate to say that there is no separate self, since everything is interdependent and in the experience of emptiness there is no separation between the absolute and its manifestation in the relative world of phenomena. Each person is a unique expression of ultimate reality who is not separate from the earth and all beings as unique expressions of ultimate reality. With realization of both our uniqueness and nonseparation, great compassion arises for the earth and all beings.

Christian insight into "Who am I?" centers on God's love. I am created by God, and I am a beloved daughter of God. I am a manifestation of God's love, and I am loved, known, accepted, and cherished by God—just as I am. Each of us is a beloved son or daughter of God and a manifestation of God's love. The metaphorical language of being a son or a daughter helps us move beyond just an intellectual understanding to the direct experience of the depth and breadth of God's love for each of us.

"Just as I am" means that you should never try to be something other than who you are as a unique manifestation of God's love. It is a mistake to think you are not good enough, that you don't deserve God's love. It is a mistake to think you must be better, or other than what you are, in order to be loved. God loves you just as you are, and in the light of that love, you flourish and grow. You express God's love by being kind and loving toward yourself and others and by developing your unique gifts for the benefit of all. You *are* God's presence and love in the world, and you are called to embody this in your relationships with others.

With respect to "What am I here for?" a Christian response is to love God and others. We are here to share God's love with others. God gives each of us gifts to share with others, and in that sense we are cocreators with God, using our gifts to create the world we live in, and to care for each other, all beings, and the earth.

Although Zen answers and Christian answers to these big life questions are different, the Zen experience of realizing the underlying unity of life and responding with love, respect, and reverence to each person and situation is not so different from the Christian experience of loving God, others, and the earth as manifestations of the living God in the world today.

The other day a person asked me, "Why do you do Zen?" I don't remember what I replied, but as I drove home, the following poem came into my mind in response to this question:

> Because I know that I am this
> This life
> This tree
> This leaf
> This mare's tail cloud in a clear blue sky
> This moment
> This day
>
> This night
> This darkness
> This star
> This whole glowing Milky Way
>
> This situation
> The whole thing
> Not turning my face from it
> All of life is this
> My original face
>
> These hands and this touching
> These feet and this walking
> These ears and this hearing
> These eyes and this seeing
> Just this

This family
These friends
This community
Everyone included

I am this
Particular and vast
Inconceivable

I don't know everything
There is so much I don't know
I stand in awe, not knowing
Yet I know that I am this

17

Radical Emptying

Sitting in zazen, we let go of all thoughts, concepts, theories, opinions, and images—the good ones along with the bad and the neutral, the profound along with the mundane. We let go of it all and sit open and present to that which is beyond thought and beyond that which can be conceptualized or imagined. We don't try to push thoughts out of the mind, but we don't intentionally think or daydream either. When we become aware that we have drifted off in thought, we simply let go of the thought and return the attention to the belly expanding and receding with the natural breathing. During meditation, thoughts come and go through the mind, and at times there are no thoughts arising. There are times of restlessness with lots of thoughts, and there are times of great clarity with few thoughts.

Zazen can be viewed as an emptying process. Letting go of our precious thoughts and opinions is difficult for many people. Often, not only are we attached to our thoughts, but we are identified with them. Due to Descartes's influence, we grew up in a culture of "I think, therefore I am." After years of schooling, we are highly intellectual, while other aspects of our humanity remain less well developed. Meditation is an opportunity to take a break from thinking, which certainly has its value, but tends to dominate and obscure who we really are.

Sigmund Freud, who had an immense influence on Western culture, identified the ego as the rational, practical part of the human personality. The ego mediates the demands of the id and superego, allowing the individual to survive and function effectively in the world. The ego is not the enemy unless it is the only way you know yourself. Thinking is not the enemy unless we cling to our thoughts or are identified with them. Duality is not the enemy; the world we live in and the languages we speak are dualistic. Nonduality transcends the division between duality and nonduality. The problem arises when dualistic divisions such as us and them, self and other, inside and outside, subject and object are the only way you perceive reality and function in the world. When you sit in meditation and empty out all these divisions, your eyes open to a larger reality, the undivided whole. Emptiness reveals a greater fullness.

When we let go of or empty out everything, we experience that which is not a thing. Ultimate reality or God is not a thing. You are not a thing. You and ultimate reality or God are not separate things. In *The Record of Transmitting the Light*, Zen Master Keizan says, "Even if you are thorough and meticulous, and by all means put an end to all things and make them utterly empty, there is something that cannot be emptied out" (Cook 2003, 235–36). In other words, when everything is emptied out, what is it that cannot be emptied out? When everything that obscures is emptied out, what is revealed? We sit open and present with, and as, this great reality.

Yamada Koun Roshi, with whom Roshi Kennedy originally studied Zen in Japan, told Kennedy that he did not want to make a Buddhist of him. He was not concerned with that. Yamada Roshi said, "I just want to empty you out in imitation of your Lord Jesus Christ, who emptied himself and poured himself out in service to others."

Paul wrote, "Let the same mind be in you that was in Christ Jesus, who, though he was in the form of God, did not regard equality with God as something to be exploited, but emptied himself, taking the form of a slave, being born in human likeness. And being found in human form, he humbled himself and became obedient to the point of death—even death on a cross" (Phil. 2:5–8). The process of kenosis, or emptying, is present in Christianity in the apophatic tradition that empties out all thoughts of God so that the heart can be open to the direct experience of God. Our self-emptying mirrors Christ's self-emptying in service to the world, and God's self-emptying in the ongoing creation of the world.

In Zen practice we engage in a radical emptying process, not only letting go of thoughts, concepts, and images, but also letting go of any sense of a separate self. In the experience of emptiness, self and subject dissolve and become transparent. The separate self is transcended. All things or objects also become transparent and are transcended as well. Emptiness is not an empty void. It is not nothing or nihilism. Emptiness includes everything. Everything is a manifestation of emptiness, ultimate reality, or God, including you, yourself. No description of emptiness, ultimate reality, or God is adequate. Without direct experience it cannot be understood. Some people open to this experience spontaneously, but most open through a path of meditation. Emptiness is the emphasis of Zen practice, going beyond the small separate self to experience ultimate reality and nonduality.

The Song of the Jewel Mirror Awareness says,

The Dharma of thusness is intimately conveyed by Buddhas
    and Ancestors;
Now you have it,
Keep it well. (*Zen Peacemaker Order Service Book* 1997, 9)

Thusness is conveyed intimately when the mind is empty and clear. It is communicated through direct intuitive experience, not through logic or reasoning. Do not waste your time sitting there trying to figure it out. Thusness is emptiness or ultimate reality manifesting everywhere, shining everywhere, in everything, including you and me, if we do not cover it up.

Clarity and emptiness are embodied in our *zendo*. We create an uncluttered space in which to sit. It is an empty room with mats and cushions to sit on, a bell to begin and end meditation periods, clappers to begin and end walking meditation, and a small table for a candle, flower, and small statue of Buddha sitting in meditation. There is nothing extra in the room. All the shoes, jackets, bags, car keys, and cellphones are placed in a nearby room out of sight. We enter and leave the zendo empty-handed. But sitting in silence together is a rich experience of thusness or intimacy—just this sitting, just this walking, just this letting go, just this presence, just this emptying, just this opening, opening to the refined subtlety we experience when we sit together. We do not sit as separate individuals, but as one with ultimate reality manifesting in each other, the earth, and all beings.

There is a koan in *The Blue Cliff Record* in which "A monk asked Chao Chou, 'The myriad things return to the one. Where does the one return to?' Chou said, 'When I was in Ch'ing Chou I made a cloth shirt. It weighed seven pounds'" (Cleary & Cleary 2005, 270). Sitting in meditation, we see that everything is ultimately empty. We see emptiness manifesting in all the things in the world, such as Chao Chou's cloth shirt. Emptiness and fullness are not separate. Emptiness, ultimate reality, or God is self-emptying, manifesting in the fullness of the world. Zazen opens us to our nonseparation from ultimate reality or God, and all creation.

In our letting go, in our emptying, we lay our burden down and experience liberation. There is a wonderful phrase in the verse to this koan about Chao Chou's shirt, which was a turning word for me when I came across it—"the pure wind of unburdening" (Cleary & Cleary 2005, 272). Emptying is not a burden; it is a release. It is freedom. It is a breath of fresh air. Letting go is easy, like simply opening your hand. We are invited to simply sit and let the pure wind of unburdening blow right through us with no resistance, no obstruction whatsoever. We are empty, transparent, clear, and free.

18

Boundlessness and Healthy Boundaries

Zen teachings about boundlessness and transcending the sense of a separate self are not meant to imply that a clear sense of self and healthy boundaries in the conventional world in which we live are not essential. When you experience unbounded ultimate reality or God's presence, you see that you, everyone, and everything in the universe is a manifestation of one God or ultimate reality. The experience of emptiness is unbounded; there are no boundaries, as far as the eye can see. You are one with all that you see.

A woman came to see me in private meetings at a Zen sesshin. She had been sitting for many years and had attended many sesshins. She asked me for any tips or suggestions I might have to help her in her practice, which was *shikantaza* or just sitting. She described what she was doing during meditation and what she was experiencing. I suggested that she bring some energy to her practice, straighten her posture when she finds herself drifting, and sit fully awake and open. The next day she came to see me again, and I could see the minute she came through the door that something had changed. Her whole demeanor was softer and brighter, and she had a certain smile. She said that, during her meditation that morning, she heard a bird singing—and at once she experienced that the singing was not outside her. In that instant, there was no inside or outside, just singing. It was a joyous opening for her. After all her years of sitting, the walls went down, and from that moment on she was transformed.

Once the boundaries between inside and outside, between subject and object, between you and the universe go down, the walls you had built around yourself for self-protection crumble completely. There is no separate self to defend and protect. There is a great sense of release, and life is fresh, vital, and sensitive.

Often in Buddhism, we hear teachings about *anatta*, no-self, no separate self, as expressions of absolute or ultimate reality. But there are also teachings about the conventional world of cause and effect that cannot be ignored. As an individual, your choices and actions have consequences for yourself and others. You need to know who you are as an individual in the conventional, relative world. You need to know and be able to express how you feel, what you need, what you value, and what you want. The absolute is the world of sameness with no separate self, and the relative world is the world of differences where each person is a unique expression of ultimate reality. Psychological health includes a well-developed sense of self and provides a necessary foundation for the spiritual work of self-transcendence. From the absolute perspective, there never was a separate self; it is an illusion. In the relative world, a clear sense of self is necessary to form appropriate relationships with others and lead a fulfilling life.

From a Zen perspective, ultimate reality, from which we are not separate, is unbounded. From a Christian perspective, God is unbounded, and God's love is unbounded. At the same time, boundaries are an integral part of creation or the relative world. I remember in school seeing microscopic images of cells, each with a cell membrane surrounding it. If there was no cell membrane forming a boundary around a cell, the cytoplasm would spread out in all directions and there would not be a functioning cell. Cell membranes are semipermeable, mediating the exchange of molecules between the cell and its environment. Some people would like to live without boundaries and feel that any boundary is constricting. However, many types of boundaries are essential for physical life on earth, for psychological well-being, and for appropriate interpersonal relationships.

Meditation is a way to get to know yourself better. When you sit down to meditate, the same thoughts and feelings may arise and fade away repetitively, day after day. Without intentionally thinking, problem solving, or adding to these thoughts, sometimes you notice patterns in the thoughts and feelings. Noticing these patterns provides insight into your needs, desires, values, concerns, and limits. In order to establish clear boundaries, you first need to be aware of your needs, feelings, values, preferences, and limits. This awareness allows you to articulate clear boundaries to others in a way that is respectful to both yourself and others. Clear boundaries unite people in harmonious relationship rather than divide them.

Appropriate personal boundaries depend on your role in a relationship. Boundaries are different in your relationships with your partner, your children, your parents, your friends, your coworkers, and people you don't know. For example, children learn from appropriate limits that keep them safe and prepare them for life outside the home. You need to be able to share responsibility and work with others and hold yourself and others accountable. This way, each person learns the dignity that comes with being a contributor to the family or group. Healthy boundaries are clear and firm, yet they are flexible, not rigid.

The necessity of healthy boundaries has moved into the forefront of people's attention these days as scandals involving boundary violations in numerous religious traditions hit the headlines. These boundary violations not only harm the victims but also the members of the tradition whose trust in their religious organization is damaged or destroyed. Victims and members ask themselves, *How can people who devoted their life to spiritual development and service be so blind to the tremendous harm they cause?*

With the ubiquitous nature of these problems, religious organizations have developed policies, procedures, and training to educate members about healthy boundaries and how to handle various types of boundary violations. Some behaviors, such as sexual misconduct involving children and rape, are not only boundary violations but also crimes that must be reported to the proper authorities.

Boundlessness does not mean anything goes. Boundlessness puts us in touch with the wisdom, clarity, creativity, and compassion needed to deal as effectively as possible with difficult and complex human problems. Vigilance and healthy boundaries help us prevent problems and recognize problems in ourselves and others in a timely manner so that we can seek help and intervene to decrease suffering.

Interspiritual practice is a way to move beyond the boundaries between religious traditions. It reduces attitudes of us-and-them. It relieves the pressure people feel when required to choose one tradition only. Interspiritual practice frees people to be nurtured and enriched by the wisdom and practices of more than one tradition. Interspiritual practice does not erase boundaries. It respects and appreciates differences among traditions while building bridges that enable us to work across religious boundaries for the common good.

19

Ignorance, Sin, and Shadow

Spiritual development in the Zen and Christian traditions requires an increasing awareness of our ignorance, sin, and shadow. In the Zen world, behavior that is harmful to self or others is attributed to greed, hatred, and ignorance, which are viewed as ingrained tendencies in human beings. The most fundamental form of ignorance is not being aware of your true identity as a manifestation of ultimate reality. Before awakening to ultimate reality, you are deluded by thinking that you are a separate, enduring self. When you awaken from this delusion, you see and feel that you are not separate from ultimate reality, and thus not separate from others and everything in the universe. The experience of nonseparation makes you less likely to behave in a way that harms others or the earth. Buddha taught by example—sitting in meditation every day—to show people the way to dispel ignorance, greed, and hatred by waking up to ultimate reality, thereby experiencing serenity and spreading peace on earth.

Instead of talking about sin as Christians do, Buddhists speak of good and bad karma. Most Zen communities recite the *Gatha of Repentance* daily:

> All the harmful karma ever created by me of old
> On account of my beginningless greed, hatred, and ignorance
> Born of my conduct, speech and thought
> I repent of it now (Still Mind Zendo n.d.)

Karma is based on the laws of cause and effect, with good thought, speech, and action resulting in positive consequences and bad thoughts, speech, and action resulting in negative consequences. Karmic consequences affect not only self and others, but the positive or negative effects of our thoughts, speech, and action ripple out to affect the world. Sometimes karma is viewed in a simplistic way, leading people to engage in good deeds in order to offset their bad deeds as if keeping a ledger. However, most Buddhists realize the complexity of karmic consequences.

Traditionally, Christianity has emphasized sin, sometimes to the extent that it overshadowed the centrality of God's love in the teachings of Jesus. Sin is going against God's laws and values, turning away from a life of loving God and others. Some denominations teach that humans are born with original sin due to Adam's fall in the Garden of Eden. Some Christians take the story of Adam and Eve literally. For others it is metaphorical, pointing toward the human propensity for selfish and violent behavior resulting from thousands of years of evolution with its genetically ingrained drive for survival.

John wrote, "If we say that we have no sin, we deceive ourselves, and the truth is not in us" (1 John 1:8). Becoming aware of the things we said or did that harmed others is the first step in acknowledging our wrongdoings. The next step is gaining insight into factors within and around us that contribute to our sinful thoughts, speech, and behaviors. We then need to assume responsibility for our choices and make changes to correct our harmful behaviors.

A prayer of confession that is prayed communally in the beginning of the liturgy in several Christian denominations includes acknowledging that we have sinned not only by what we have done but also by what we have left undone. This is the tremendous challenge of Christianity: not only to avoid harming others but also to embody God's unbounded love toward others and the earth. We fall short of this ideal, but acknowledging this shortcoming keeps us always moving toward making love a reality everywhere.

Shadow is a term that comes to us from the work of Carl Jung in the field of psychoanalytic psychotherapy. Jung was a pioneer in integrating psychology and spirituality to expand our understanding of humanity. According to Jung, each person has a shadow that consists of repressed, unconscious parts of the personality. Usually, the individual considers these repressed needs, interests, and desires to be negative; therefore, they are placed out of sight in the unconscious. The shadow includes feelings and impulses that the individual's religious tradition, culture, or family considers unacceptable. The problem with the shadow is that the unconscious, repressed material tends to leak out or be acted out by the individual, without conscious awareness of what is causing the problematic behavior. Without conscious awareness of the problem's source, the individual may feel a lack of control over the behavior. Psychotherapy is indicated if the shadow or unconscious material is causing significant problems for the individual or others, but Zen, Christianity, and meditation are not forms of psychotherapy. Individuals with psychological problems need to be referred to professionals in the field who are trained to assess the many physiological and psychological factors that may be contributing to the individual's issues.

Sangha and spiritual community are essential in helping us become more aware of our ignorance, sin, and shadow. Community members give us feedback about problem behaviors that we may not recognize on our own. Part of our spiritual practice is to listen to and consider seriously the feedback that community members give us. Our ability to get along with others and to be a contributing member of the group are signs of our spiritual maturity.

Self-compassion is important with respect to ignorance, sin, and shadow. None of us are perfect, nor will we ever be. My generation was naïve in thinking that enlightenment or spiritual development would free us from ignorance, sin, and shadow. Our eyes have been opened to the fact that this is not the case. As human beings, we all make mistakes. We need to do everything we can to avoid mistakes, especially those that can have serious consequences for ourselves and others. However, when we make a mistake it is necessary to acknowledge our role in the problem, take corrective action if possible, identify contributing factors, and learn all we can from the situation to decrease the likelihood of repeating the mistake in the future. When we have done all of this, we need to let it go rather than allow it to weigh us down and prevent us from being fully alive, loving self and others.

Kristin Neff, a psychologist who has conducted extensive research on self-compassion, encourages us to be as kind and compassionate to ourselves as we are to our friends when faced with personal inadequacies, mistakes, failures, and difficult life situations (see Neff 2011). She suggests treating ourselves with kindness rather than self-judgment and criticism. Rather than withdrawing or feeling isolated during difficult times, she encourages connecting with others through a sense of our common humanity, realizing that everyone at times makes mistakes and feels sad and discouraged. Neff recommends mindfulness meditation to become aware of our thoughts, feelings, and problems, without being overidentified with them. She combines Western psychology and Buddhist teachings to put us in touch with the bigger picture.

In Zen and Christianity, the bigger picture is ultimate reality or God manifesting in human beings and in the world in an infinite number of ways. Harmful or destructive behavior on the part of humans is influenced by multiple factors, such as our neurophysiology, life experiences, culture, choices we make, drugs, alcohol, war, poverty, and the interaction of innumerable additional circumstances. We must embrace our complexity as human beings as a reflection of the inconceivability of ultimate reality or God. There is much that humans do not know, but in not knowing, we are open to do our best, not denying difficult aspects of ourselves, and responding to each person and situation we encounter in life with wisdom, kindness, and love.

20

Impermanent, Interdependent, Interconnected

My neighborhood is in a valley with mountains on both sides and a stream running through the nearby woods. I love to walk along the stream. When I get to a place where the streambed is filled with rocks and boulders, the water picks up speed and the sound is delightful. I sit there for a while listening to the turbulence and rush of whitewater over stone. It's soothing and refreshing. It is a lesson in impermanence as the water wears its way through rock.

In the woods, as I walk past fallen trees worked by moss and bugs, crumbling back into earth, it is clear to me that everything is impermanent. In this age of increased ecological awareness, it's easy to understand that we are interdependent with plants, animals, people, and the planet's entire ecosystem. We are dependent on the quality of the air we breathe, the water we drink, and the food we eat. What the other billions of people on the earth are doing affects us all. In that sense, we are all interconnected. On an intellectual level alone, there is tremendous value in understanding our impermanence, interdependence, and interconnection.

However, Zen meditation takes us beyond an intellectual acknowledgment of the truth of impermanence to the direct experience. As we sit in meditation with attention on the breath, we notice each breath as it comes and goes. Each breath comes to us only once; it will never come back again. Thoughts come and go. Feelings come and go. Sounds come and go. We awaken to each moment of life, never to come again. Realizing the changing nature and impermanence of life brings a sense of immediacy, freshness, and vitality to life each moment.

The direct experience of the impermanence of life awakens us to the futility of clinging. Buddha taught that selfish clinging, rather than embracing life just as it is moment by moment, is the cause of unnecessary suffering. Acceptance of the existential truth of impermanence liberates us from grasping and clinging and frees us to savor each fleeting moment of life.

On Easter morning at the empty tomb, Mary Magdalene encountered the risen Christ. At first, she did not recognize him, but then he called her name, "Mary!" She instantly recognized him and replied, "Rabbouni!" (teacher). He said to her, "Do not hold on to me" (John 20:16–17). Sometimes this is translated as "Do not cling to me." We cannot hold on to or try to recapture what was in the past—in Mary's case, her beloved teacher—no matter how profound or wonderful the person or experience was for us. We must let go and open ourselves to the present, arising fresh and new.

Zen emphasizes that we cannot try to grasp or cling to any experience or insight we have, no matter how profound and precious it may be. Zazen is sitting in meditation with an open mind, not clinging—letting go of thoughts, no matter how interesting or alluring. We don't take the bait and join the thought or try to hold on to it. We just let go of any intentional thinking, reminiscing, or problem solving and sit fully present to what is here now. Clinging is stagnation and death. If we try to hold on to the past, we miss each moment of life as it flashes before our eyes.

Roshi Kennedy has a beautiful work of calligraphy that Yamada Roshi made for him that hangs on the wall at Morning Star Zendo. It says, "Fundamentally, not one thing exists." When you experience this for yourself—that everything is ultimately insubstantial, that everything is an expression of emptiness—then your own impermanence becomes clear to you here and now.

You are liberated from trying to cling to life, and you are freed to appreciate life fully in each moment.

Many Christian denominations sing a familiar doxology praising the Trinity that says, "Glory be to the Father, and to the Son, and to the Holy Ghost. As it was in the beginning, is now, and ever shall be, world without end. Amen." This brings to our awareness that along with the ever-changing tides of life, there is a great reality that is beyond space and time, that is not a changing thing, that is not a thing at all, that is not a concept or thought, and that endures now and forever.

Zen helps us take this a step further to be a direct experience by asking us, "When was *in the beginning*?" If we sit long and hard, opening to the depth of this reality, we can experience for ourselves that the beginning is always right here and now. Where else could it possibly be? Each moment is a flash of creation, never to come again. Each moment we are a flash of creation, fresh and new.

Each year I go out for a walk in the first snowfall of the season. This year as I walked with big fluffy snowflakes falling around me, I thought, *Look at these beautiful snowflakes. Not one of them asks about eternal life.* All we can do is drink in the fleeting beauty of life, fully aware of how precious it is.

Western psychology has emphasized autonomy as the hallmark of mental health. With the dominance of this view, often our dependency needs are denied and repressed. It is okay to huddle, hug, nurture, and be nurtured throughout our life, so long as we don't cling. Autonomy and individuality need to be balanced with acknowledging our dependence on each other so that we can live in harmonious interdependence with one another, able both to give and receive. This balance comes with the realization of the impermanence of life and our interconnection with each other, the universe, and beyond.

There is a growing awareness, supported by scientific research, that body, mind, and spirit are interconnected. Zen meditation helps us experience this as a fact. Zazen is not thinking about life. It is sitting in an alert and awake posture, paying attention with the whole bodymindspirit. This leads to the realization of no separate self, no subject observing objects, and oneness with distinctions. Zen refers to this as *intimacy*. This is not an intellectual experience in the head or mind. Interactions with other people and with the environment are felt on a visceral level, making interdependence and interconnection a direct experience.

"Keichu Makes Carts" is the koan that helped me most directly experience impermanence, interdependence, and interconnection. The koan says, "Keichu made a hundred carts. If he took off both wheels and removed the axle, what would he make clear about the cart?" (Yamada 1990, 44). First, it shows that all the parts are interdependent and interconnected; that's how a cart functions. The koan also makes it clear that sooner or later everything in this world comes apart. Carts don't last forever. Parts don't last. Everything is impermanent. Every person is impermanent and will pass away.

In this koan, ultimate reality or wholeness takes the form of a cart. Sitting and working with this koan, you experience for yourself that even when all the parts are taken away, the unmade, uncreated, boundless whole remains. Koans aren't logical or linear; they help you take an intuitive leap into wholeness, your own wholeness. You see directly that you and everything else are the functioning of the whole. In Zen, this is sometimes called the *great functioning*. Seeing deeply into impermanence, interdependence, and interconnection, you are liberated into wholeness. You leap from fragmentation, separation, separation anxiety, and desperate clinging into the direct experience that you are already whole. Even in the midst of everything coming apart in your life, there is also a deep sense of wholeness. I especially like Zen Master Mumon's comment on this koan: "If you can realize this at once, your eye will be like a shooting star and your spiritual activity like catching lightning" (Yamada 1990, 47).

21

The Particular

Zen and Christianity teach us to value both the universal and the particular. Vast ultimate reality or the infinite inconceivable God manifests in the particular. We know and love the inconceivable by appreciating and embracing the particular.

To experience the emptiness of all things is essential in Zen, but we don't stop there. It is just the first step, the beginning. We go on to experience emptiness manifesting in all things. The formless takes form. Emptiness and form are not two separate things. Sound is silence moving in the world.

One Saturday at one of our New River Zen Community *zazenkai*, or days devoted to meditation, Tom was sitting with the group in the zendo, in the basement of the house into which Charles and I had just moved. It was a windy mid-May day, and Tom noticed that he was flooded with feelings from his boyhood, growing up in Nebraska along the Platte River. Suddenly he realized what was triggering his feelings: the rushing sound of the wind passing through the huge cottonwood tree outside the zendo window. He recognized this distinctive sound, the rushing and rustling of wind in the cottonwood leaves, unlike the hum of the wind in the pines, or the sharper sound of the wind blowing through oaks. In the spring, when the cool wind from Canada came down through Nebraska on its way from North Dakota to Oklahoma, the cottonwoods along the river made a rushing sound, just this sound, like no other.

You are a unique manifestation of ultimate reality or God. You are of immense value to your parents, your own child, brother, sister, friend, and lover. You are irreplaceable. I experienced this every day working as a nurse. A parent sitting by the bedside of his or her child wants to know every detail of the child's condition. Are there any changes in the lab values? What is my child's temperature? What medications is my child receiving? The parent wants to be sure everything possible is being done to bring comfort and healing, as it should be. This particular child is what matters most.

Christianity teaches that God has unbounded love for each of us, for you and for me. Jesus told the crowd who came to hear him, "Are not five sparrows sold for two pennies? Yet not one of them is forgotten in God's sight. But even the hairs of your head are all counted. Do not be afraid; you are of more value than many sparrows" (Luke 12:6–7). You are never forgotten or abandoned, although you may feel that way at times. Do not be afraid. God loves you always. Your life matters. God loves and cares about every particular detail of your life, the life of each and every person on earth, all of the animals, and the land itself.

When you lose someone close to you, you miss his or her particular way of walking across a room, that person's tone of voice, smile, face, hands, and reassuring touch. It is hard to say good-bye. You grieve and honor your loved one's unique life on earth. You share pictures and stories from the person's life. Some people place a tombstone on the grave and visit at certain times of the year, like my cousins Dianne and Mary Jane who go every year on Memorial Day to place fresh flowers on their parents' graves. Roshi Kennedy said that he would like to be cremated and his ashes spread on the earth to help grow a tree. Each person has his or her own preferences in life—and many have preferences for after life—and these should be honored when possible.

A koan in *The Blue Cliff Record* states,

> Emperor Shukuso asked Chu Kokushi, "When you are
> a hundred years old, what shall I do for you?" Kokushi
> answered, "Make a seamless pagoda for this old monk."
> The emperor said, "I should like to ask you, what style is
> it to be?" Kokushi remained silent for a while. And then
> he said, "Do you understand?" "No, I do not," said the
> emperor. (Sekida 2005, 194)

In this exchange, the emperor is asking National Teacher
Kokushi what kind of monument the emperor should build in
Kokushi's honor after he dies. Kokushi's reply, a seamless pagoda,
indicates that he does not want a monument built of wood, stone,
and mortar. Seamlessness points toward ultimate reality. The best
way for the emperor to honor Kokushi is to realize his own nonseparation from ultimate reality and thus everything else in the
universe, that he is a seamless whole. The emperor doesn't know
what Kokushi means because he has not experienced the seamless, undivided whole—his own true nature, ultimate reality. This
awakening is what Kokushi wishes for the emperor, to awaken
and embody this realization. Kokushi wants the emperor to *be*
a seamless pagoda instead of him building one. He wants the
emperor to continue his practice of meditation and see ultimate
reality for himself.

This is what Kokushi wants for each of us too, to experience
seamlessness or ultimate reality, and embody it, express it, each
in our own style. He does not request one particular style. Each
person's awakening experience is unique, and each of us is called
to express it and live it out in our own particular way. This is the
infinite creative impulse of life or ultimate reality as it manifests
in the world.

There is a story in all four Gospels, although the details vary
from one to the other, about a woman John named Mary who
brought a jar of very expensive perfumed oil to a dinner that Jesus
was attending, and she anointed him with it. Two of the Gospels
even say that she rubbed it on his feet and dried it off with her

hair. People attending the dinner chastised her for wasting money on the expensive oil, money that could have been used to help the poor. Jesus told them to leave her alone, that she has done a beautiful thing. Jesus explained, "For you always have the poor with you, and you can show kindness to them whenever you wish; but you will not always have me" (Mark 14:7).

Jesus does not mean to minimize the urgency of helping the poor, but he is emphasizing that it needs to be balanced with appreciating those closest to us and expressing our love to them while they are still with us. Mary's anointing of Jesus was a pure act of love and an expression of her appreciation for his unique presence with her in that moment. Jesus tells her and all those present at the dinner that she will always be remembered for this act of love and kindness to him.

I always enjoyed hearing the story that my mother often told about the time my father came home on leave from serving overseas in the army during World War II. They were engaged at the time and had been apart for over a year, only able to keep in touch through letters they sent to each other. The moment he arrived home, still in uniform, he went straight to Brockport College, where my mother was in French class at the time. When she saw him, she was thrilled! She jumped to her feet and they fell into each other's arms, hugging and kissing while all the girls in the class clapped and cheered. The French teacher, who was originally from Paris, cried. As he sobbed, the teacher said that he was eternally grateful to all the American soldiers for the role they played in the liberation of Paris from Nazi rule.

Roshi Kennedy often says, "We cannot put our arms around the formless." We can only put our arms around those we love, and when we love others, we love God. We know and embrace God in the particular.

22

Being Selfless

Both Zen and Christianity emphasize being selfless. Buddha taught that selfish clinging is the cause of unnecessary human suffering and that selflessness is the antidote. He pointed the way to end suffering by experiencing the emptiness of all things, including your sense of a separate self. You see that you are distinct, but not separate from ultimate reality and the whole universe. You are a manifestation of empty oneness. This is not a thought or theory. It is an intuitive experience that Zen meditation facilitates. During meditation, you let go of all thoughts and concepts and sit open to that which is beyond all thoughts, words, and images. With the direct experience of emptiness, it becomes clear that there is nothing to cling to and no one who is clinging. You experience that you and everything you see are one. In the realization of the oneness of life, great compassion arises for all. This takes form in the bodhisattva ideal not to enter nirvana until the grass itself is enlightened.

In Christianity, we become selfless by accepting God's boundless love. God pours out his love in all creation. We are a manifestation of God's love. We are God's love in the world and are called to share this love with others. When asked about the greatest commandment, Jesus not only said to love the one God with all your heart, soul, mind, and strength, but also "You shall love your neighbor as yourself" (Mark 12:31). This does not just mean treating your neighbor like you wish to be treated. It is a call to love your neighbor, and to see and feel that—as manifestations of God's love—you and your neighbor are one. This is what is meant by loving your neighbor as yourself.

The Apostle Paul said, "I have been crucified with Christ; and it is no longer I who live, but it is Christ who lives in me" (Gal. 2:19–20). We can interpret what Paul is saying to mean that he has died to his separate ego-dominated self. He is resurrected or awakened to a new sense of self that is one with Christ and one with God and all creation. Selflessness is liberation from the domination of the separate ego self that is never satisfied. It is awakening to a life of boundless love, united *with* God and *as* God in the world. Being selfless is a life of fullness and love.

Christians reach out to others from this sense of fullness and love. The Christian ideal of selfless service is not based in self-deprivation or self-deprecation. In your daily life, you are to take care of yourself and develop your God-given gifts so that you can love, serve, and care for others and all creation.

As a wonderful hymn titled "I Surrender All" says,

All to Jesus I surrender,
All to Him I freely give;
I will ever love and trust Him,
In His presence daily live.

What is freely surrendered to Jesus is the ego, that part of the self that wants to control and call all the shots in life. This is similar to the Buddhist idea of letting go of selfish clinging and transcending the sense of a separate self or ego. In this sense, we become selfless or egoless. When we are egoless, ultimate reality or God is revealed.

Ananda was Buddha's cousin, born on the day of Buddha's awakening. Ananda was exceptionally bright, and it was said that he remembered every word of all the Buddha's sermons. However, Buddha's disciple Mahakashyapa first had an awakening experience and became Buddha's successor. Ananda was

Buddha's attendant until Buddha's death, and then he became Mahakashyapa's attendant. One day, "Kashyapa called, 'Ananda!' Ananda replied. Kashyapa said, 'Knock down the flagpole in front of the gate.' Ananda was greatly awakened" (Cook 2003, 36). Awakening is an intuitive experience that comes when we let go of all thoughts and ideas. Ananda had such a brilliant intellect that it was a hindrance rather than a help in intuitive awakening. Traditionally, a flagpole and flag were put up by a monastery's front gate when there was a dharma debate or lecture. When Mahakashyapa said to Ananda, "Knock down the flagpole in front of the gate," he was calling out to Ananda to let go of even the slightest thought and to surrender the ego completely. With this surrender, Ananda was awakened and subsequently became Mahakashyapa's successor.

From the absolute perspective, there is no separate self whatsoever. In the relative or conventional world, there is an individual self. The ego allows the conventional self to make rational decisions and function effectively in life. A well-developed sense of self is necessary for human survival and well-being. The experience of being selfless or egoless needs to be integrated with a well-developed conventional self for human flourishing and a life of selfless service for the liberation and flourishing of all.

Being selfless is not a grim life of self-sacrifice and self-denial. It is the absence of selfishness, self-indulgence, and self-centeredness, none of which brings us a deep sense of peace and joy. Being selfless, we are concerned about the needs of others and engage in compassionate action to help people in need and care for the earth and all beings. We do not do this to gain merit or for self-aggrandizement. We do this out of love, from the insight that sees and feels one's neighbor *is* oneself.

Being selfless does not require that you give up the simple pleasures of life, like the closeness of family, conversation with a friend, a good cup of coffee, a walk on the beach, a swim in the lake, a picnic at the park, a warm shower, or watching a sunset. In fact, it is necessary to do things like this, to have plenty of love and beauty in your life. One day, Charles and I were at Roshi Kennedy's apartment in Jersey City. He put the theme from the movie *Romeo and Juliet* on the stereo, and as he went out the door to go to work, he said to us, "Fill your mind with this! Fill your mind with beauty."

Being selfless requires that you make sacrifices in order to help others, but you must be careful not to deplete your resources and lose your ability to be helpful to anyone, including yourself. Give from a life of fullness, not of lack. Realizing your oneness with ultimate reality or God, you see that there is nothing that you lack.

23

No Other, Only Other

There are two koans in *Gateless Gate* that I call sister koans because they go together hand in hand. In Case 30, "Taibai asked Baso in all earnestness, 'What is Buddha?' Baso answered, 'The very mind is Buddha'" (Yamada 1990, 148). Hearing these words, Taibai experienced a great awakening and went off to meditate in the mountains for about thirty years to deepen his realization.

In Case 33, "A monk asked Baso in all earnestness, 'What is Buddha?' Baso replied, 'No mind, no Buddha'" (Yamada 1990, 161). Subsequently, the unnamed monk is off hiking in the mountains and runs into Taibai. The monk tells Taibai that he studies Zen with Baso. He tells Taibai that Baso's teaching has changed and that these days he is teaching "No mind, no Buddha." Taibai replies, "He may say, 'No mind, no Buddha' as he will, but for me it is, 'The very mind is Buddha' forever" (Yamada 1990, 162). When the monk reports this encounter to Baso, Baso says, "I see the plum has ripened!" (Yamada 1990, 162–63). The name *Taibai* means big plum, and Baso's comment is acknowledging the ripening of Taibai's realization.

These two koans underscore the fact that Zen has no party line. There is no imitation in Zen. Each person's realization is unique, fresh, and original. You see it and express it in your own way. Ultimate reality or God is one, but an individual's experience and expression of it varies from person to person. For some, the emphasis stays the same over time, as was the case for Taibai. For others, the emphasis may shift.

Some people experience awakening as the realization that "I am not separate. I am everything I see! I am one with ultimate reality, and thus I am all that I see. When I see my friend, the friend I see is me. Nobody else sees my friend the same way I do. The world I see reflects my mental and emotional state. In this sense, I create the world I see. I am the mountains, trees, lake, and breeze. With this realization I am liberated to enter into life without separation and free to experience it fully. I am truly intimate with myself, others, and the earth beneath my feet. There is no other."

This is the view from an absolute or ultimate perspective. Of course, the realization that there is no other needs to be integrated into everyday life where you and everyone else you meet also have individual identities. Expanding your vision beyond the limits of a separate self and conventional reality adds infinite depth, richness, and intimacy to life.

The Zen classic *The Three Pillars of Zen* describes the enlightenment experience of an American woman. After years of daily zazen and attending multiple sesshins, she attended a sesshin led by Yasutani Roshi. She was working intensely on the koan Mu when suddenly she plummeted to the depths of Mu and broke through to see emptiness for herself, to see it and be it. The next morning, she met privately with Yasutani Roshi to present her insight into Mu. He asked her various questions and affirmed her realization. He told her, "Now you understand that seeing Mu is seeing God" (Kapleau 1989, 265). It was clear to her that she truly understood.

Another way to say, "Seeing Mu is seeing God," is to say, "It is clear to me that everything is God." This reminds me of an interview with Reverend Murray Rogers regarding his friend Swami Abhishiktananda. He told how Swami Abhishiktananda, a Dominican priest, once said to him, "Murray, is there anything but God?" (Rogers 2006).

We can flip 180 degrees and go from saying, "There is no other," to saying, "There is only other." Here we enter into the inconceivability and utter mystery of ultimate reality or God. Some people describe this as God's absolute transcendence. When we encounter another, we bow in reverence and awe, knowing that we are standing on holy ground.

In the Gospel of Mark, it says that as Jesus was dying on the cross, darkness came over the whole land from noon until three. At three in the afternoon, "Jesus gave a loud cry and breathed his last. And the curtain of the temple was torn in two, from top to bottom" (Mark 15:37–38). This refers to the veil or curtain in the temple in Jerusalem that separated the people from the Holy of Holies. The barrier or separation between God and humankind was torn in two, removed completely, through Jesus's love and sacrifice. Followers of Jesus open themselves to the wholly other by following his example, living a life of love, sacrifice, and service for others. From the beginning, we are not separate from the other, but through Jesus we open our hearts to become aware of that which is utterly beyond our comprehension. Ultimately, there is only other.

There is a Zen story in *The Blue Cliff Record* about Huang Po coming to meet Zen Master Pai-chang for the first time. "Pai-chang said, 'Magnificent! Imposing! Where have you come from?' Huang Po said, 'Magnificent and imposing, I've come from the mountains.' Pai-chang asked, 'What have you come for?' Huang Po said, 'Not for anything else'" (Cleary & Cleary 2005, 73).

Charles shared with me three experiences he had working with the koan "Not for anything else." The first took place during a Zen retreat. He was doing zazen in the zendo when the teacher said, "If not this, then what?" The phrase kept repeating in his mind. Then the phrase stopped and there was only the sound of the cicadas singing. There was not anything else, only the cicadas. It was as if he had never heard that sound. When it came time for meetings, he walked up the stairs to see the teacher, and there was just walking up the stairs, not anything else. Entering the room to demonstrate his insight, he felt he could have done or said anything, because there was not anything else. The positive way to say "not anything else" is *just this*. Everything is *just this*; not anything else. This is the direct experience of nonduality.

His second experience occurred years later. While he was taking a walk, out of nowhere, everything collapsed. Time collapsed. There was only this moment, not anything else. There was no yesterday or tomorrow. He said, "Actually there was not even this moment separate from me." Space collapsed. There was only this point and not anything else. He said, "It was an experience of myself as this point that had no dimensions and no parts. Movement stopped, no coming or going. I should mention that *experience* is not the correct word for these events since experiences come and go."

His third experience occurred about a year later while he was doing zazen at home. There was a sense of fragile presence, neither personal nor impersonal, neither himself nor other. A whisper arose within him: "What have you come here for?" He replied, "Not for anything else." Then Charles asked, "What have *you* come here for?" And the whisper came, "Not for anything else."

Part IV

Meditating and Praying

24

Meditation as Prayer

Since the beginning of my Zen meditation practice many decades ago I have viewed meditation as a form of silent prayer, a way to open more fully to ultimate reality or God. This is and has always been my primary motivation or intention in meditating daily. The great commandment of Jesus to "love the Lord your God" requires quality time spent awake and aware in God's presence. Meditation is an act of love. Sitting in the deep silence and stillness of meditation, there is not one hair's breadth of separation between God's presence and my presence. It is one glorious refined presence. Meditation breathes new life into me, giving me the strength to be God's presence in the world in the circumstances of daily life.

While opening to God or ultimate reality is my primary motivation or intention for meditation, I want to be clear that this does not mean I am thinking about God, philosophizing about ultimate reality, or meditating on religious matters during this time. In meditation, we let go of all thoughts and images no matter how sublime they may be. Meditation is taking a break from all directed thought and sitting open to direct encounter with that which is beyond all concepts, all description, or anything we could imagine.

Today, many people are practicing various types of meditation, such as mindfulness, for secular reasons such as decreasing stress, anxiety, pain, and depression, or increasing mental focus and performance. While these aims are worthy, Zen meditation is not a means to an end. It is not a tool, skill, or technique. Zazen is a type of mindfulness that can have positive physical, mental, and psychological effects, but these are side effects. Ultimately, zazen is an expression of who we are at our deepest level. This nondual insight has power to heal that extends far beyond the relief of symptoms. It is an intuitive realization of wholeness and nonseparation from others, the world, the universe, and ultimate reality that transforms one's life.

Zen Master Kuie-feng Tsung-mi, who lived in China during the eighth and ninth centuries, classified Zen meditation into five categories (Fischer-Schreiber et al. 1991, 70). These categories remain relevant to us today as meditation becomes widespread in our culture. The first category, Bonpu Zen, is zazen practiced for secular reasons such as physical or mental health. The second category, Gedo Zen, is zazen that is practiced for spiritual reasons that are outside the context of Buddha's teachings and insights. This category of zazen includes people who practice zazen to gain supernatural powers. Shojo Zen, the third category, is zazen practiced for inner peace and individual liberation. Shojo Zen is the province of many Buddhists who believe in reincarnation and meditate in order to liberate themselves from the cycle of rebirth. The fourth type of Zen, Daijo Zen, moves beyond a focus on individual liberation toward the insight that there is no separate self. Acting from the realization of the oneness of all beings and the great earth, the individual works for the well-being and liberation of all.

These first four categories can be viewed as reasons or motivations to practice zazen. The final category, Saijojo Zen, refers to zazen that is not practiced as a means to an end. The means and the end are one. Zazen is an expression of the Way, the great reality, or your own original nature. Zen Master Dogen referred to this type of Zen when he emphasized that zazen *is* enlightenment. In this sense, zazen is not goal-directed or purpose-driven. Zazen transcends a cause-and-effect orientation altogether. It is an expression of unboundedness and limitless possibilities right here and now.

Delineating these five types of zazen is helpful in elucidating the fact that all types of meditation are not the same. The practice is not the same, and the results are not the same. This understanding is especially important for people who are combining different spiritual traditions, such as Zen and Christianity. A person sitting silently in zazen as a form of Christian contemplation or Christian meditation might be considered an example of Gedo Zen, which is meditation with a religious motivation, but one that lies outside the context of Buddha's insight and teachings. On the other hand, a Christian practicing Zen with knowledge of both Christian teachings and Buddha's insight and teachings; sitting silently in zazen beyond thoughts, concepts, and images; and open to breaking through the illusion of a separate self and experiencing ultimate reality for the benefit of all beings is an example of the fourth or fifth category of Zen. This practice is consistent with Buddha's highest teachings and with Jesus's highest teachings, which I call *nondual Christianity.*

In speaking of meditation as prayer, I am highlighting the religious or spiritual aim of the meditator in sitting in silence, awake and alert. The spiritual intention, although we are not intentionally thinking about it—or anything else for that matter—during meditation, changes the practice and the experience.

My Zen teacher, Roshi Robert Kennedy, who is also a Jesuit priest, says prayer is "to come into the presence of ultimate truth without intention, with reverence and love." In meditation, we sit in silence, awake and alert to the presence of ultimate reality, which is not separate from, or other than, our own ultimate reality or presence. We sit with humility and reverence acknowledging that, although we are not other than this great reality, God or ultimate reality is a greater reality that transcends our human capacity to know intellectually. We pray without thoughts, words, concepts, or images, and are open to listen rather than to speak. We sit with awe in the presence of that which is incomprehensible and indescribable. Yet there is an intimacy in this presence. We are at home and can sit without tension, completely relaxed, accepted, and loved. Love, peace, and joy naturally arise.

Silent prayer, such as meditation, is not the only kind of prayer, but for some people it is their main or preferred type of prayer. During one of our group discussions following zazen at our weekly New River Zen Community meeting, Carol said that for her, the silent, wordless prayer of zazen is the kind of prayer she likes best because "When I pray with words, it seems like I'm telling God what to do." In zazen, there is no begging, pleading, bargaining, or demanding. We are not overly disappointed when things don't go the way we hope.

This issue brings to the fore the basic attitude of acceptance that is an aspect of Zen meditation. We sit open to whatever arises during meditation, yet we don't intentionally engage in thinking or daydreaming. We accept ourselves as we are, and our life as it is, without trying to push away the difficult aspects or cling to the positive. Zazen is sitting open and alert without any agenda. It is a way to embrace and wordlessly embody the phrase from the Lord's Prayer, "Thy will be done."

When we let go of thoughts, words, preconceived ideas, and endless expectations, we find ourselves present, free, and open in new ways to experience God or ultimate reality. I do not mean thinking about God or ultimate reality in new ways, but rather experiencing. Nothing is added to the simple act of sitting silently and still, paying attention to the breath, the posture, or just sitting. This prayer of silent sitting each day brings peace, presence, and the perspective of oneness to life. It refreshes and renews me like taking a shower in the morning. It's an essential part of my daily routine. I would not feel as clear or function as well without it. There is a refined subtlety to zazen that is beauty beyond description. It helps me see the beauty of life that has always been here.

25

Who Prays to Whom?

The nontheistic nature of Buddhism and Zen leads one to ask, "Do Buddhists and Zen practitioners pray?" and if so, "Who do they pray to?" These are complex and deep questions. First, it is important to say that there are many different types of Buddhism and many flavors of Zen with different practices and styles of prayer. Second, although most people who practice Zen are Buddhists, an increasing number of Zen practitioners also practice another religion, usually the one in which they were raised. They do zazen plus pray in accord with the religion to which they belong. Third, some people who practice Zen are not Buddhist, nor do they practice any other religion. Yet many Zen practitioners who do not belong to any religious tradition pray. For most Zen practitioners, silent meditation is their major but not their only form of prayer.

At most Zen centers, there are daily services in which the community honors Buddha and the lineage of teachers and prays for the needs of community members and the wider community. During the service, they bow, offer incense, and chant sutras together. The service includes the dedication of the merits of their practice to Buddha, bodhisattvas, and others. During the service, prayers take the form of affirmations or the expression of good wishes for the well-being of others, such as those who are ill. An example of this type of prayer is, "We pray for the health and well-being of all those afflicted by diseases of body, mind, or

119

spirit. . . . May they be serene through all their ills, and may we realize the Enlightened Way together" (*Zen Peacemaker Order Service Book* 1997, 19). The services include an invocation such as,

> The Absolute Light, luminous throughout the Whole Universe, Unfathomable excellence penetrating everywhere;
> Whenever this devoted invocation is sent forth it is perceived and subtly answered. (*Zen Peacemaker Order Service Book* 1997, 19)

An impersonal ultimate reality is invoked, one that perceives and responds in subtle ways. The universe, or the totality, perceives and responds to our prayers. Other invocations call forth Buddhas and bodhisattvas.

Christian prayers are addressed to God, such as "Our Father who art in heaven." Some Christians pray to Jesus, Mary, saints, or guardian angels, and through them to God. I most often begin my prayers with "Dear God." For me, God is ultimate reality or the highest reality, and I address my prayers to the One God. Other names I sometimes use are Inconceivable God or Infinite God. Although God is beyond my comprehension, I believe God hears and responds to our prayers. Jesus often prayed, and when he did, he prayed to God the Father, who he called "Abba, Father" (Mark 14:36). He encouraged the people to pray, saying, "Ask, and it will be given you; search, and you will find; knock, and the door will be opened for you" (Matt. 7:7).

From a nondual perspective, the person praying and the one prayed to are not separate; they are one. Jesus was one with the Father, yet he prayed to the Father. In Zen, we are not separate from ultimate reality; we experience that we are a manifestation of ultimate reality. In prayer, ultimate reality that has taken form reaches out to ultimate reality that is greater than any particular form. The particular reaches out to the totality; the totality hears and responds. As a manifestation or creation of God, the Christian reaches out to the transcendent God who is greater than all creation.

This is the power of prayer: to acknowledge and connect with that which is greater than the small, separate self or ego. Opening to that which is greater than the sum of all creation puts the ego in its proper perspective. That is why members of twelve-step programs such as Alcoholics Anonymous ask their higher power for help in overcoming addiction. The ego is out of control with respect to alcohol or other substances or behaviors, and the person reaches out to something greater, to something or someone beyond the limited ego. For some, this is God; for others, it is ultimate reality; and for some others, it is the power of the group.

We see the ego in perspective to that which is greater in Zen paintings. Often the mountains loom large above the tiny houses, boats, and villagers. Prayer is a form of devotional surrender to that ineffable mystery that we are, and at the same time, is infinitely greater than the small ego self. This allows us to live in harmony with self, others, and nature while opening heart and mind to that which is infinite and inexpressible.

This great reality is so vast that it embraces paradox—immanent yet transcendent; personal and impersonal; no other, only other; merit and no merit; not one, not two. Bodhidharma told Emperor Wu that there was no merit accrued for his good deeds, yet in Zen services, the merit of the Zen practitioners' prayers and practice is dedicated to others. Even though ultimately there is no merit, all good thoughts and actions have positive effects on you, and the positive effects ripple out to affect subtly the whole universe. Dedicating the positive effects of your good thoughts and actions to others is a way to practice selfless service. It is a way to develop positive habits and keep the ego from becoming inflated. From an absolute viewpoint, there is no merit. There is no cosmic bank account where your merit is accumulated. However, in a relative sense, every kind action has a positive effect, and every selfish or unkind deed has a negative effect. Prayer is a way to practice kindness and help this kindness spread throughout creation.

Ultimate reality or God is inconceivable, indescribable, and ineffable, so in meditation, we sit in the presence of this great reality in silence, beyond words. But this great reality also transcends silence. It takes form in you and me and everything we see. It takes form in words, thoughts, images, gestures, and facial expressions. It takes form in human words and in the songs of birds. Words and silence are not separate. Song and silence are not separate. They are one great reality. Meditation is a way to experience this clearly for yourself and transcend the duality of speech and silence. This nondual realization frees you to pray with both words and silence.

Often in the Christian tradition, prayer is defined as communicating with God. Some repeat prayers they have learned, and others engage in their own words in a heartfelt conversation with God. Some emphasize listening more than speaking. While all of the above are fine at times, I think of prayer more as spending time with God, of being with God. Growing up, I was definitely a "daddy's girl." My father worked long hours as an engineer, and I cherished the time he was at home when I could be with him. He wasn't a psychologically or spiritually expressive person, so most of the time we spent together was not spent in conversation. He was a builder, and so often I was on standby in case he needed me to run and get a tool or hold the other end of a board. We enjoyed just being together, which typically took the form of us sitting at the kitchen table, on the front porch, or in the living room together, each reading a book and drinking iced tea. There was a special intimacy and happiness in this simple act of just being together.

This is how prayer is for me, the simple act of just being with God, in silence, in conversation, or in each ordinary act of daily life. Intimacy and happiness come with a life of prayer. Zen meditation has allowed me to dive deeply into this act of being with God to see clearly that there is no separation between me and God. God is my very being.

26

Simple Prayers

When we pray with words, it is best to keep it simple and brief. Too many words tend to cover over or obscure rather than bring to the fore our intimacy with ultimate reality or God. We can pray in our own spontaneous and heartfelt words, or use words from Scripture, liturgy, koans, songs, or poems that come to us as powerful prayers, turning the heart toward God or ultimate reality. We may begin with words, and then words may fall away.

We do not intentionally pray with words during our sitting meditation time. Zazen is a time of silent, wordless prayer—a time set aside each day for opening to that which is beyond all thoughts, words, concepts, and images. But at other times during the day and night, we can pray with words as the spirit moves us, aloud or silently, alone or with a group, informally or formally in liturgy.

One clear summer day walking through the hills surrounding my home, I felt a refreshing breeze against my cheek and the prayer spontaneously arose, "Thank you for the wind on my face." Then the prayer became just the sensation of wind on my face. Then it became just this walking, just this presence—no words, just intimacy.

My prayer while walking with the wind on my face reminded me of the following verse in *The Gateless Barrier*:

The wind moves, the flag moves, the mind moves:
All of them missed it.
Though he knows how to open his mouth,
He does not see he was caught by words. (Shibayama 2000,
    209)

We can be caught by words, but words can also set us free.

A very short prayer that I find helpful is "Fear not." This message appears many times in both the Hebrew Scriptures and in the New Testament. In Isaiah, it says, "Do not fear, for I am with you" (41:10). In Luke, the angel Gabriel appears to Mary and says, "Do not be afraid . . . for nothing will be impossible with God" (1:30–37). The book of Revelation says, "Do not be afraid; I am the first and the last" (1:17). This simple prayer, "Fear not," is a powerful reminder that we stand in the presence of vast, ultimate reality, or infinite God, who is greater than all the adversities of life. It is a prayer that allays fear and brings courage, strength, and comfort. This prayer allows you to release your fears and trust in the inconceivable God. It is a prayer of liberation. Rather than being immobilized by fear and anxiety, it frees up your energy so that you can return to a positive, life-affirming state of being.

Each day I pray the Lord's Prayer because this is the prayer that Jesus taught the disciples when they asked him to teach them to pray. I also frequently pray a single phrase from the Lord's Prayer, "Thy will be done." This is a prayer of surrender of the ego to God, who is greater than the small ego self and beyond its comprehension. This prayer reinforces the nondual realization that "Thy will is my will."

Another favorite nondual prayer of mine is "There is no God but one" (1 Cor. 8:4). This prayer affirms the experience of the ultimate oneness of God and God's manifestation in all creation. I am one with God and all creation.

A simple prayer for harmony and balance that I have carried with me ever since the days I lived on the Navajo reservation is "May I walk in beauty." This prayer restores harmony with the earth, all beings, the community, and ultimate reality or the Great Spirit. It frees me to move through life with grace and balance.

Zen liturgies contain chants that help us raise the awakened mind. A line that I frequently use as a short prayer is "May the mindflower bloom in eternal spring" (*Zen Peacemaker Order Service Book* 1997, 15). In this context, *mind* refers to the Chinese character *hsin*, which means not just mind but also heart, spirit, consciousness, and Buddha nature. It means awakening to our oneness with ultimate reality. It is a prayer that calls us to awaken to the timelessness, fullness, freshness, and beauty of life right here and now.

There is a koan in which "Every day Master Zuigan used to call to himself, 'Master!' and would answer, 'Yes!' Again, he would call, 'Thoroughly awake! Thoroughly awake!' and he would answer, 'Yes! Yes!'" (Yamada 1990, 62). I sometimes borrow this prayer from Zuigan, asking myself, "Are you awake?" and then I answer, "Thoroughly awake!" This prayer is a call to attention and a reminder of who I am and what is primary in life. Also, this koan contains a one-word prayer, "Yes!" This is a total "Yes!" to life, come what may.

The "thoroughly awake!" part of this koan reminds me of Jesus praying in the garden at Gethsemane. Jesus is in great distress and asks his disciples, Peter, James, and John, to stay awake and pray with him. Jesus then goes a short distance away to pray. Three times he returns and finds the disciples asleep. He says, "So, could you not stay awake with me one hour?" (Matt. 26:40). I use this as a prayer of motivation to energize my meditation practice at times. "Can you not stay awake with me for one hour?"

One of my favorite hymns is W. W. Walford's "Sweet Hour of Prayer." It sings of the sense of relief and joy experienced with spending time with God in prayer.

With such I hasten to the place
Where God my savior shows His face.

For me, just the words "sweet hour of prayer" bring to mind the warmth and sweetness of prayer that call me to set aside time to be present with ultimate presence or God. These words motivate me and call out to my soul. My life is not complete and balanced without time for meditation and prayer.

In addition to special time set aside for prayer each day, I pray frequently throughout the day. For example, working as a nurse and nursing professor, each time I enter the hospital I say a prayer: "Dear God, please bless this great house of healing and heal every patient here today. May I be a healing presence to each patient I take care of today. Please don't let me make any mistakes or do anything that would cause harm. In Jesus's name I pray. Amen." Nursing is challenging work that takes all your intellect, clinical competence, communication skills, humanity, presence, and spiritual resources. Prayer is a powerful way to be alert, fully present, and connected with those spiritual resources.

I often pray when I encounter great beauty. For example, one full-moon night in my backyard I prayed, "Bathed in moonlight, I am moonlight." It was a simple prayer of joy at recognizing my own original face in the moonlight.

Some prayers are funny. Often when I rode through the busy streets of New York with three Sisters of Saint Joseph of Peace, Janet, Rosalie, and Mary, we would sometimes narrowly escape a fender bender and one of them would exclaim, "Jesus, Mary, and Joseph, enlighten us, aid us, and save us!" It was a lighthearted way to call out for help and at the same time send out a prayer for enlightenment. I thought it was very apropos for a carload of people who were deeply engaged in both Christian and Zen forms of meditation and prayer.

During his agony on the cross, Jesus prayed a prayer from the Psalms: "Father, into your hands, I commend my spirit" (Luke 23:46). I intend to pray this prayer when my death is near. It is a final surrender into the arms of a loving, inconceivable God. I sometimes pray a version of this prayer now. "God, I rest in your arms." This prayer brings great comfort, release, and peace.

27

Praying with the Body

As noted in chapter 3, whenever I teach someone who is new to Zen how to meditate, I begin with the proper posture for Zen meditation. When the body sits up straight and tall, not slouching or leaning against the back of a chair or wall, the mind follows suit and becomes more awake and alert. You sit awake and alert, not just with your mind, but with every cell of your body. In this sense, meditation is praying with the whole body. The body is enlivened by correct posture and an increase in energy that helps you sit still and pay attention. It takes some time to get used to sitting comfortably for twenty-five minutes in this erect, but not rigid posture. However, once you get used to it, it is slouching that feels uncomfortable. Sitting up straight—fully awake and balanced—feels natural and healthy.

Paying attention to your breathing, as your belly expands with the in-breath and flattens with the out-breath, gets you out of your head and into your body. When your mind wanders off in thought, you just let go of the thought and bring your attention back to the belly gently rising and falling with your natural breathing. Thoughts carry you off into the past or future, but the body, breath, and posture are touchstones to the present. When you become more experienced in meditation, you may not need to focus on the breath, but rather bring your attention back to the posture, or just to sitting and remaining open, awake, and alert. When the body settles in silence and stillness, the mind settles

too. Body and mind are not separate. You become deeply relaxed
and at the same time alert and attentive. In the deep stillness of
meditation, the mind opens to that which is beyond thought and
imagination. You awaken not only to your whole body but to the
One Body.

Some of us raised in the West don't think of the body as a
gateway to the spirit. We don't think of the body itself as a manifestation of ultimate reality. Consequently, we get lost in thought,
theorizing, and speculation, causing us to miss life and spirit even
as we embody, breathe, eat, and walk it. The Zen sutra *The Identity of the Relative and Absolute* says, "If you do not see the Way,
you do not see it even as you walk on it" (*Zen Peacemaker Order
Service Book* 1997, 8).

During days, weekends, or weeks of extended meditation, sitting meditation is alternated with periods of walking meditation.
Just as sitting meditation can be viewed as a type of silent prayer,
walking meditation is a type of moving prayer. For some people,
walking meditation is even more powerful than sitting meditation—just walking together single file, they feel one with the flow
of life. During walking meditation, when the mind wanders off
in thought, we let go of the thought and bring the attention back
to the sensation of the feet coming in touch with the ground,
or to the sensation of moving, or to the rhythm of walking. I
always like the feel of the early-morning mist on my skin when
we do walking meditation outside. The body comes to life, the
One Body—the people in line, the earth beneath our feet, the trees
and bushes, and the sky extending out to the ends of the universe.

During sesshin we eat together in silence. Before eating, the
bell rings and we chant the mealtime *gatha*, or prayer, together.
Eating is a continuation of meditation, so it can be considered
prayer too—chewing, tasting, and smelling prayer. Zen Master
Rinzai once said,

> Followers of the Way, mind is without form and pervades the
> ten directions.

In the eye it is called seeing, in the ear it is called hearing.
In the nose it smells odors, in the mouth it holds converse.
In the hands it grasps and seizes, in the feet it runs and carries.
Fundamentally it is one pure radiance; divided it becomes
    the six harmoniously unified spheres of sense. (Sasaki
    2009, 165)

Ultimate reality takes form in every action of the body, and when we are aware of this radiant reality, every action is a prayer.

The most profound moment of prayer for many Christians is receiving the bread and wine, the body and blood of Christ, in Communion. We eat the bread and drink the wine, taking Christ into our own body. The community gathers to share this holy meal. Eating together, the One Body of Christ is nourished. Christ is embodied in the community as the members go out into the world to love and to serve.

Zen and Christianity both engage in the practice of bowing to embody an attitude of reverence to that which is greater than the individual. Christians bow their heads to pray and sometimes kneel in prayer. Zen practitioners frequently bow to Buddha, to their teachers, to each other, to the Zen hall, and to the cushion they sit on to meditate. Bowing acknowledges and honors ultimate reality, which is embodied in each of us and in everything we see. It cultivates an attitude of caring not only for human beings but also for everything in the environment around us which not only serves us, but also has intrinsic value as a manifestation of ultimate reality and as a member of the One Body. Bowing is also a gesture of humility and a way to free oneself from domination by the ego.

Zen practitioners and Christians use similar hand positions for prayer. Christians join the hands' palms together in prayer in a position very similar to the Zen *gassho* position. In Zen settings, much can be communicated through placing the palms together in gassho—welcome, respect, reverence, humility, and farewell. Palms together in this gesture embody the nondual perspective of "not one, not two."

In many Christian churches, prayer is embodied in song, dance, and drama. I recently attended an Easter pageant at a local church. It was deeply moving on a visceral level to see, hear, and feel the life, death, and resurrection of Christ present around you on stage and throughout the sanctuary. About sixty men, women, and children of all ages were dressed in costumes, singing, dancing, and acting out scenes of Jesus healing, preaching, praying in the Garden of Gethsemane, being crucified on an actual life-size cross, and appearing as the risen Christ. Praying with the body through song, dance, and drama has an effect on the bodymind-spirit that words alone do not.

The Song of the Jewel Mirror Awareness says,

> When the wooden man begins to sing,
> The stone woman gets up to dance;
> It's not within the reach of feeling or discrimination—
> How could it admit of consideration in thought? (*Zen Peacemaker Order Service Book* 1997, 11)

We are more than our thoughts, words, or feelings. Prayer with the body moves us beyond the intellectual or psychological levels to help us take an intuitive leap to awaken with every cell of the body to ultimate reality, manifesting in our every breath, song, step, and gesture.

In recent decades the emerging field of neuroscience has rapidly expanded our understanding of the functioning of the human brain and its effects on the body, mind, emotions, and behavior. This body of knowledge needs to be integrated into our understanding of meditation and prayer without reducing meditation and prayer to a science, devoid of the spiritual depth of these practices. There is initial research supporting mindfulness meditation, which includes Zen meditation, bringing about changes in the structure and function of the brain associated with positive effects on behavior and well-being (see Tang et al. 2015). There is tremendous potential for advancing human development through the integration of scientific knowledge about the physiological and psychological effects of meditation and prayer with wisdom from the world's great religious traditions that developed these practices. This integrated knowledge base needs to be developed using both quantitative and qualitative research methods in order to gain in-depth understanding of the interaction of physiological, psychological, and spiritual aspects of meditation and prayer.

28

Prayers for Help

In good times and in hard times, I pray to God for help. Jesus taught the people to pray to God the Father for their daily needs, saying, "Give us this day our daily bread" (Matt. 6:11). Even though God already knows what we need before we ask, this prayer keeps us focused in the present on the needs of this day and not preoccupied with the future. It does help us to be satisfied with our basic needs being met, not lost in an endless list of wants and the discontent this engenders. This prayer also places the ego in proper relationship to God, who is greater than we are, and with all God's creation on which we depend for our basic needs.

As a nursing professor, I was frequently asked to write letters of recommendation for students who were applying for jobs. Many of the hospitals required me to fill out a checklist in addition to making written comments. An item often included in these checklists was "Seeks help when needed." This was considered a positive quality, and understandably so, since nurses often need help to move a patient, to clarify an order, or to draw on the knowledge of a more experienced nurse. It is far safer to check and be sure rather than guessing or pretending you know more than you do. Being willing to ask for help is a strength not just in nursing but also in life in general.

Praying to God for help acknowledges that there is much that we do not know. It breaks through the delusion that the ego has everything under control. There is much in life over which we have no control. Praying for help means that we do all we can to help ourselves and others, and then we surrender the rest to a higher power, to God. This does not minimize our responsibility to do all we can, but it frees us to let go of what we cannot control. In seeking help from God, we are released from carrying the weight of the world on our shoulders.

Buddhists also pray for help. They pray to the highest reality, the totality, and the totality hears and responds. Sometimes they pray to ultimate reality in the form of Buddhas and bodhisattvas. Once I was at an American Zen Teachers Association meeting at the Vermont Zen Center and was deeply moved by the way they chanted *The Lotus Sutra Scripture of Kanzeon Bodhisattva* with elaborate *taiko* drumming to keep time. Kanzeon is the bodhisattva of compassion. The chant lists numerous terrible situations from which recalling the power of Kanzeon will rescue us, such as,

> If someone wants to hurt you
> And pushes you into a great fire-pit,
> If you think on the power of Kanzeon
> The fire-pit will turn into a pond. (Vermont Zen Center
>   2008, 5)

The chant reminds us in times of trouble to draw on the power of Kanzeon, which is her boundless compassion. In our oneness as a manifestation of ultimate reality, we, like Kanzeon, are also manifestations of boundless compassion. We can draw on this limitless spiritual resource when we find ourselves in difficult situations.

When I was in eighth grade, I had a friend who told me that she did not believe in God. I asked her in all sincerity, "If you don't believe in God, then who do you turn to when you need help?" Without a moment's hesitation she said, "My mother." She and her mother were both wonderful people, and I understood how this was true for them. I too was fortunate to have a mother to whom I could turn for help when I needed it, but from a young age I also realized that many things were beyond the scope of what my mother or I could manage. Throughout my life, I have felt the need to turn to a higher power, which for me is God.

On the night before his crucifixion, Jesus went to the Garden of Gethsemane with his disciples to pray. Knowing what lay ahead for him, he was in agony and prayed intensely. The Gospel of Luke reports, "In his anguish he prayed more earnestly, and his sweat became like great drops of blood falling down on the ground" (22:44). As Jesus knelt in prayer, he said, "Father, if you are willing, remove this cup from me; yet, not my will but yours be done" (Luke 22:42).

Jesus shows us how to pray when we face life's most trying times, times when we are in agony and anguish, whether for ourselves or loved ones. He shows us how to pray earnestly, sincerely, and intensely. He shows us that it is okay to feel overwrought or distraught. Even Jesus experienced this depth of despair. We can be confident, as Jesus was, in asking God for what we need. At the same time, we remain open to God's will, which is beyond our understanding. We pray to God for the strength to meet life's greatest challenges with courage and love.

Buddhism has a form of meditation or prayer called *metta*, which means friendliness or loving-kindness. You offer well-being to yourself and others, saying,

> May you be happy.
> May you be safe.
> May you be healthy.
> May you be at ease. (Salzberg 2016)

First, sit comfortably with your eyes closed and say these phrases to yourself. Then bring to your mind someone who was kind to you at some time in your life and slowly repeat these four phrases to that person. Next, picture a neutral person in your life, perhaps someone you occasionally see at work or when you are out doing errands. Repeat the four phrases wishing happiness, safety, health, and ease to this neutral person. Next, picture someone in your life who you find difficult in one way or another. Repeat these four phrases with this difficult person in mind. Then picture all the people in the world and repeat these four phrases, wishing well-being to everyone. Conclude the meditation by picturing all beings and wishing them happiness, safety, health, and ease. This meditation helps us connect with all people in that we all share these common human needs and desires for happiness, safety, health, and ease. This prayer also helps us realize that love is boundless and there is no limit on the goodwill we can offer to ourselves, others, and all beings.

I attended a workshop for therapists and social workers in Roanoke, Virginia, where Sharon Salzberg led the group in loving-kindness meditation. I had done this type of meditation several times at various retreats over the years and always found it meaningful and positive. However, this time when I did the loving-kindness meditation with the group, the phrase "May you be at ease" stood out. After decades of Zen practice with its emphasis on paying attention, I realized that I had never really heard the part about "be at ease." I also had the sense that this was partly coming from my childhood. My father, rather than making a request, often barked out orders like a drill sergeant. To some extent, this reflected the child-rearing practices of the time, and some of it was because he was a sergeant in the army during World War II and he was using his previously learned skills to establish order in a household with four children. When I heard, "Be at ease," it was like I had been stuck for many years on the order for "Attention!" and now I finally heard the order, "At ease." Hearing those words, I sighed, and a certain type of tension left my body and has not returned. Attention is essential, but it needs to be balanced with ease.

I have adapted my daily prayers based on metta meditation. First, I pray to God that my family be healthy, safe, kind, loving, and joyful. Then I offer this prayer for myself, then for my friends, and then for all people everywhere. I end with prayers for the environment and all beings, for world peace, and for freedom for all the earth's people.

29

Prayers for Forgiveness

Forgiveness is a major teaching in Christianity. Jesus says, "For if you forgive others their trespasses, your heavenly Father will forgive you; but if you do not forgive others, neither will your Father forgive your trespasses" (Matt. 6:14–15). If we refuse to forgive those who hurt us, we imprison ourselves within the walls of anger and animosity. God frees us when we open our hearts in mercy to those who have harmed us. We are set free by God's mercy and love within us. Ultimately, we are a manifestation of God's mercy and love. Our realization and embodiment of this insight help break the chains of evil and ignorance in the world.

Forgiveness means letting go of past hurts. It means not holding a grudge or seeking revenge. Zen meditation is helpful in this regard. When we sit in meditation, we notice thoughts and feelings as they arise and dissipate, and we let go of them, returning our attention to the breath or to just sitting. Over and over, the mind wanders off in thought, storytelling, or daydreaming, and over and over, we let go and come back to the present, just breathing, just sitting. Zen meditation is largely a process of letting go. As we exercise our capacity to let go, our letting go becomes quicker and stronger. This frees us to be present here and now and to open to something larger than the small, separate self.

People often resist the idea of forgiving someone who has harmed them or a loved one, because they think forgiving means forgetting. When we forgive, we let go of our anger or vengeance toward the offending person, but we do not forget. We need to remember what happened and learn from the situation so that we can prevent the problem from happening again in the future and causing further harm.

Buddhists view greed, anger, and ignorance as three poisons. In forgiving, we are letting go of anger. Holding onto anger has a negative impact on our own physical and emotional health, increasing stress, anxiety, and depression. Holding onto a grudge, and the story we tell ourselves over and over about the person who offended us, fuels our anger and causes greater harm to ourselves than to the person who harmed us. This does not mean that we should repress or deny our anger. We feel and acknowledge anger without adding to it by repeating it over and over in the mind, allowing it to take over way too much of our time and energy. We notice the anger arise and dissipate in the light of our attention. We neither repress nor reinforce it. We simply release our grip on it and let it go. Forgiveness is letting go of anger toward those who hurt us and taking back more and more of the fullness of life in the present.

Sometimes people resist forgiving the person who harmed them because they think that forgiveness means that a relationship with that person needs to be reestablished. Forgiving a person who harmed you means letting go of past hurts and the desire to get revenge or bring harm to the other person. It does not mean that you have to be in a relationship with the person. In some circumstances, forgiveness indeed leads to a new and improved relationship with the person who harmed you. However, in many circumstances a person you have forgiven does not change his or her behavior or attitude significantly, so a relationship with the person would likely lead to further harm. In these situations, we wish the offending person well and rely on others, including those with professional training, to help this person change and grow, especially in order to prevent any harm inflicted on others.

Jesus said, "Do not judge, so that you may not be judged. For with the judgment you make you will be judged, and the measure you give will be the measure you get" (Matt. 7:1–2). We need to make judgments every day to ensure the safety and well-being of self and others. We also need to act on those judgments to prevent harm. However, Buddhism teaches us to be compassionate, and Christianity teaches us to be merciful in our judgment of others.

Compassion and mercy are the measures we want for ourselves when we intentionally or unintentionally harm another, so these measures are the ones we need to use in our interactions with those who harm us. Many complex situations demand great wisdom to discern what is the most compassionate, merciful, and loving thing to do for all concerned. We need to acknowledge that God or ultimate reality is the ultimate judge and healer. We cannot forgive and heal by ourselves. We do our best to judge, forgive, and heal, but we do not know all the factors contributing to an individual's behavior; moreover, we do not know how to fix many complex human problems. We pray to God or ultimate reality to help us forgive and be compassionate. We do our best to forgive, and then we release the person who harmed us into the care of God or ultimate reality.

Sometimes it is easier to forgive others than it is to forgive yourself. When you do something that harms others or yourself, the first step is to admit your error and learn from it, so that you don't repeat it. Christians pray to God for forgiveness and to seek the strength and wisdom needed to change. Each morning in Zen centers, the *Gatha of Repentance* is chanted. In this prayer, Zen practitioners repent of all evil karma committed through their conduct, speech, and thought. In addition to praying about our errors and making a commitment to change, when possible, we need to make amends or restitution to the person we harmed. When we have done this, it is time to let it go and not ruminate about it or carry it around with us forever. Not forgiving yourself is a form of selfish clinging, which Buddha taught is the cause of unnecessary suffering. From a Christian perspective, we let go and gratefully accept God's gift of forgiveness.

In Zen we embrace the Three Pure Precepts: cease from evil, do good, and do good for others. Each day I use these precepts as a prayer that is short and simple, yet for me it is powerful:

Dear God,
Please forgive me for the harm I have done
and the good I have failed to do.
Please help me to do no harm
and do good for others.

This prayer helps me accept God's forgiveness, let go of past shortcomings, and commit anew to doing no harm and doing good for others this day.

Sometimes when people suffer serious trauma or losses in life, they become angry with God. They don't understand how God could allow something so terrible to happen, and they ask, "Why me?" Here it becomes necessary to admit that we do not know. There are no adequate explanations. God or ultimate reality is larger than our human ideas about goodness and justice. God or ultimate reality is beyond our human capacity to comprehend. We bow down to that which we cannot know. In letting go of our small ideas about God or ultimate reality we are able to forgive ourselves, others, and God. In forgiving, as difficult as it may be, we embrace and are embraced by the inconceivable.

30

Prayers of Gratitude

Being grateful is a fundamental spiritual attitude, and prayers of gratitude are a way to express and cultivate this quality of heart and mind. Through gratefulness we become aware of and reduce one of the three Buddhist poisons, namely, greed. Greed is also one of the seven deadly sins in the Christian tradition. When we express gratitude for what we have, we counteract our human tendency to want more and more. Wanting more than we need and always what is new on the market is constantly reinforced by advertising and our consumption-based culture. Such greed leaves us wanting; it breeds discontent. Saying prayers of gratitude is a spiritual practice that cultivates contentment and alleviates the suffering we needlessly generate for ourselves by always wanting more. In expressing gratitude for what we have, we embrace life as it is, and our energy is available to make life the best it can be.

Offering prayers of thanks is not something to reserve for Thanksgiving dinner once a year. We can benefit from offering thanks at every meal, even when we are eating on the run, a commonplace these days. In this case, we can simply pause, take a breath, and say, "Thank you God for this food and for all who grew and prepared it. May I be nourished by this meal so I can serve and love others throughout this day." It is also a valuable practice to say grace when we share a meal with family or friends to express thanks for our food and for each other. This affirms your bond and establishes a positive habit. It acknowledges our dependence on God and our interdependence on each other and all creation.

At mealtimes during New River Zen Community's days of meditation and longer retreats, we ring the bell three times and then chant together the following traditional meal gatha:

> First, seventy-two labors brought us this food,
> we should know how it comes to us.
> Second, as we receive this offering, we should consider whether our virtue and practice deserve it.
> Third, as we desire the natural order of mind, to be free from clinging,
> we must be free from greed.
> Fourth, to support our life, we take this food.
> Fifth, to attain our Way, we take this food. (Village Zendo 2019)

The meal gatha expresses our appreciation for all the work that went into preparing the food we are about to eat. It helps us reflect on our relationship with food, so we don't eat excessively out of greed. The meal gatha brings to our attention the need to eat healthfully so that we can do the work of meditating and opening to ultimate reality for the benefit of ourselves, others, and the earth.

Working as a nurse taught me to be grateful for almost everything. Caring for patients who struggled to take each breath, I became grateful for each breath I take with ease. Caring for patients with heart problems, I became grateful for the regular rhythm of my heart beating in my chest, not too fast and not too slow. Caring for patients who could not eat, I realized what a gift it is to be able to chew, swallow, and digest my food. Taking care of patients who could not walk, I appreciate each step I take without the need for assistance. Each of our senses and functions is miraculous, and I am in awe of the complexity of the human body. Each day I thank God for my health, for the health of my family, and for the miracle of my life. Appreciation for the gift of health puts other problems into perspective and makes me grateful for what truly matters in life. Gratitude raises our awareness of the extraordinary nature of the ordinary.

Each morning and evening at Zen centers, we make three profound bows to Buddha and the Zen ancestors, including our own teacher, for keeping Zen alive in the world and for making it available to us. Our gratitude is expressed with the body as we bow down on our knees, bringing the forehead to the ground in front of us, then raising the hands several inches off the ground on either side of the head, and lowering them back down to the ground. In making these profound bows, the whole body is offered as a prayer of gratitude. We also offer incense to Buddha and the lineage of teachers. In offering incense, the sweet fragrance of gratitude permeates life here, there, and everywhere.

When my great-great-great-aunt Anna Howard Shaw corresponded with her mentor, Susan B. Anthony, the closing Susan B. Anthony used at the end of one of her letters was, "With unbounded love and faith" (Shaw 1915, 235). Inspired by this, I often end the letters I write to my Zen teacher, Roshi Robert Kennedy, with the closing, "With unbounded gratitude and love." This expresses the depth of gratitude I feel for my Zen teacher and for the insights with which I have been blessed as a result of his guidance in Zen practice. Throughout my twenty-five years of schooling, I had many good teachers, but I never had a mentor or anyone who could help me learn what I most deeply wanted to know and experience. A Zen teacher embodies the teaching and teaches by example. This is how we learn in the spiritual sphere of life. The phrase "unbounded gratitude and love" reflects my experience that, at its deepest level, gratitude *is* love. Prayers of gratitude are prayers of love.

As followers of Jesus we bow down and give thanks to Jesus Christ, who is our teacher. By example, and through his words, he taught us that the one God is a loving God. He showed us how to walk the path of love in this world. Through prayers of gratitude, we open our hearts to God's infinite generosity, and we say thank you, most of all, for the gift of love.

Many in the field of positive psychology, such as Martin Seligman, recommend keeping a gratitude journal, and each evening, just before going to bed, taking the time to write down five things from the day for which you are grateful (see Seligman 2002). Research supports this practice as a way to improve your health and happiness. Although this is a positive exercise and habit to establish, I prefer prayers of gratitude because, in addition to the benefits that come from expressing gratitude, prayers open me to ultimate reality or God and place gratitude in a broader context. Even in times of trouble, I am grateful for God's love. Often, I give thanks for intimacy with ultimate reality or God, and for the many ways that ultimate reality manifests in the particular.

> Thank you, God, that my family and I are healthy and safe.
> Thank you for my friends.
> Thank you for this crystal-clear drink of water that is delicious and thirst-quenching.
> Thank you for time to rest in my warm, comfortable bed.
> Thank you for the freedom that we are blessed with in this country. May all people around the world have freedom.
> Thank you for all the opportunities I have had and for those that lie ahead.
> Thank you for the infinite blessings you give to me each day.
> Thank you for your unbounded love.
> For you, I am truly grateful. Amen.

31

Prayers of Praise and Awe

In the Christian tradition, we praise God with psalms, songs, and prayers. The Psalmist tells us, "It is good to give thanks to the LORD, to sing praises to your name, O Most High" (Psalm 92:1). We raise our voices in praise to God, and bear witness to the highest reality that surpasses all things. The book's final psalm says, "Let everything that breathes praise the LORD!" (Psalm 150:6). We join the whole creation in giving praise to the highest reality that manifests in each and every one of us. This raises our awareness and unites us in our true identity as God's presence in the world.

I had a wonderful boss and friend, Janet Boettcher, who was a nurse for many years, including service as a nurse in the navy during the Vietnam War. She wrote a million-dollar grant to obtain a mobile clinic so that the nursing faculty and students could provide health care in rural Craig County in the mountains of Virginia. She raised one son and three foster sons and often shared with me not only her nursing expertise but also motherly child-rearing advice. She was the wife of a Baptist minister, and she was loving and expressive about her faith. When she died suddenly in her fifties, I attended her funeral, and we sang her favorite hymn, Fanny Crosby's "Blessed Assurance." The refrain to this hymn is, "This is my story, this is my song, praising my savior all the day long." This song of praise perfectly expressed her life of warmth, generosity, service, and love of God. She praised God in word and deed by the life she led each day. I learned much from her about praising God.

Songs and prayers of praise are a cataphatic approach to God that articulates what God is and celebrates God's positive attributes. The apophatic Christian tradition approaches God as the inconceivable highest reality that is beyond all words and concepts. God is approached not through words and songs but through silence, opening us to the awe and wonder of the inconceivable God. Apophatic and cataphatic practices can be integrated to expand and enrich our spiritual life.

Zen leans more toward the apophatic approach in its emphasis on silent meditation as the path to realizing ultimate reality, which is beyond words, concepts, and images. *The Song of Zazen* says, "The zazen of the Mahayana is beyond all words of praise" (Village Zendo 2019). However, it goes on,

> Boundless and free is the sky of Samadhi,
> Bright the full moon of wisdom,
> Truly, is anything missing now? (Village Zendo 2019)

In this context, the word samadhi refers to the experience of emptiness, which has no characteristics and no separate subject and object. Although this experience is ineffable, Zen points to ultimate reality using metaphor and verse. To me, these are words of praise and awe.

Zen Master Yun-yen said to Tung-shan Liang-chieh, "Don't you know that the Amida Sutra says, 'Streams, birds, and trees all praise the Buddha and praise the Dharma?'" (Cook 2003, 196). When Tung-shan heard this, he experienced awakening and exclaimed, "Wonderful! Wonderful! The preaching of the Dharma by the nonsentient is inconceivable" (Cook 2003, 193). Everything, whether sentient or nonsentient, is a unique manifestation of ultimate reality, and in its own particular way, it praises the great reality.

"A monk asked Hyakujo, 'What is the most wonderful thing?' Jo said, 'I sit alone on this Great Sublime Peak'" (Sekida 2005,

216). The majesty and beauty of nature, such as tall mountain peaks, trigger awe and wonder in people of all ages and cultures. The jagged peaks of towering mountains are breathtaking, especially when we first behold them. Their vastness expands and refreshes the spirit. We can break down Hyakujo's response to the monk's inquiry about the most wonderful, the most sacred, or the highest truth. Hyakujo says, "I sit." To be able to sit in meditation like a great mountain is wonderful indeed! He says, "I sit alone." In sitting, he experiences oneness. He is saying, "I am all one. I am not separate from ultimate truth and the whole universe. I am whole. I am complete. There is nothing that I lack. This is the most wonderful thing!" The great sublime peak is a metaphor for unbounded awareness or the infinite manifesting as a mountain peak, all of nature, and you and me. Zen uses story and metaphor, but most of all the sitting itself, to praise and lead us to the direct experience of that which is most wonderful and awe-inspiring of all.

Each year in mid-May, New River Zen Community rents the retreat house at Alta Mons, a Methodist retreat center about an hour from home. The retreat house sits beside a stream that runs down through a valley between two mountains. We who live here in the mountains go deeper into the mountains for a weekend of silent meditation together. The silence of the weekend is accentuated by the fact that the mountains block all the cellphone signals, so no one is even tempted to glance at a cellphone while there. Swift water flows down from the mountains over huge boulders lining the creek bed, making an unending rushing sound that washes away thoughts and worries as we sit all day in the roaring silence and fresh air of the open-windowed zendo. We do our walking meditation outside down a long lane that runs along the creek. When the sun sets, the grassy meadows surrounding the retreat house and the trees lining the lane come to life with hundreds of lightning bugs flashing bright points of light. It is magical and magnificent, and we are filled with awe and wonder as we walk silently, single file, into the night.

There is a well-known Zen story about a monk who just arrived at the monastery to meet with Zen Master Xuansha. The monk said,

> "I've just arrived here and I beg the master to point out a gate whereby I may enter."
> Xuansha said, "Do you hear the sound of the water in Yan Creek?"
> The monk said, "I hear it."
> Xuansha said, "That's the place of your entry." (Ferguson 2000, 275)

The whole creation is a song of praise, the sound of a mountain stream, the bark of a dog, the cry of a baby, the laughter of children, the rustle of leaves, your own heartbeat. Right here is the place of entry into the awe and wonder of ultimate reality or God. Do you hear it? Enter here.

After I take the family dog, Roscoe, out on his leash for a walk around the neighborhood, I let him off his leash when we get back to the backyard. He immediately runs like the wind at full stride around the backyard several times and then leaps over the steps onto the deck ready to go inside. What a magnificent creature he is when he runs free. I call him Roscoe the Wonder Dog. It is like unleashing the power of prayer and experiencing God's awesome and immeasurable magnificence and omnipotence.

32

Unceasing Prayer

The Apostle Paul urges the followers of Jesus to "Rejoice always, pray without ceasing, give thanks in all circumstances; for this is the will of God in Christ Jesus for you" (1 Thess. 5:16–18). This raises the question "How do we pray without ceasing?" For some, this means to pray always, every morning and evening, with short prayers interspersed throughout the day. Others use prayer beads and repeat a short prayer or phrase like "Lord Jesus Christ have mercy on me" over and over until it is deeply embedded in the heart and mind. Another approach is simply to hold Jesus in your heart and be open to God's presence throughout the day and when awake at night. Many do some combination of these prayer forms and, in addition, participate in daily or weekly liturgy, praying with the Christian community.

In recent decades, mindfulness has gained widespread attention, primarily as a way to reduce stress and thereby improve physical and mental health. Zen meditation is a form of mindfulness, but rather than being used for stress reduction, it is aimed at transcending the sense of a separate self and opening to ultimate reality. As such, it is a spiritual practice and can be viewed as a form of silent prayer. Mindfulness—whether secular mindfulness or mindfulness as a spiritual practice—involves awareness in the present moment with an open, nonjudgmental attitude. During sitting mindfulness meditation, when we notice that the mind has drifted off in thought, we let go of the thought and bring the attention back to the breath, to sounds in the environment, or to just sitting awake and open in the present. In mindfulness as a form of silent prayer, we sit present to ultimate reality, which manifests in our own presence. It is a prayer of presence, a presence that is unceasing.

Mindfulness is a practice that does not end when the bell rings at the end of a meditation period. When we get off the mat, we can be fully present in whatever we are doing. When we walk, we let go of thoughts and allow our attention to be on the sensation of walking, not lost in what we need to do next. When we are planning, our full attention is on planning. When we do the dishes, the attention is on just washing and rinsing the dishes, the warm soapy water, the clear rinse water, and the sparkling clean dishes in the dish drainer. When we are attentive, open, and not preoccupied, every action of daily life becomes a prayer of presence, open to ultimate reality or God manifesting, sparkling, in and around us.

One day at work I noticed a flyer on the bulletin board announcing that a Buddhist priest, Claude Anshin Thomas, would be coming to campus to give several talks and lead a day of mindfulness meditation at Selu Conservatory, a retreat center owned by the university. I had met Claude several times over the years at events sponsored by Bernie Glassman's Zen Peacemaker Order and at one of our annual American Zen Teachers Association meetings and wondered who, other than me, would know of him down here in southwestern Virginia and make the arrangements for him to be a guest speaker and retreat leader for the university community. I discovered that he was invited by the Military Resource Center at Radford University. Claude was a helicopter gunner in the Vietnam War and leads mindfulness retreats for veterans like himself who have PTSD. Some of the programs he provided while on campus were specifically for active military and veterans, geared to the particular needs of this group of students.

Claude showed up at Radford University in the clothes he always wears, full Buddhist robes. His attendant, also in Buddhist robes, carried a small gong with her, and at random times, about once per hour, she rang the gong. Claude immediately stopped whatever he was doing or saying and paused for a moment of silence. This is a practice he learned from Thich Nhat Hanh to remind us to be mindful throughout the day. Claude shared with the group that due to his time in Vietnam, he cannot simply walk across the main quadrangle like all the students strolling down the sidewalks to their next class. He is hypervigilant, scanning the rooftops of the buildings for snipers and feeling an urgent need to take cover to avoid being a moving target out in the open. To cope with this anxiety, he repeatedly brings his attention back to the present. For him, mindfulness is a survival strategy and a spiritual practice that heals the wounds of war.

In the spirit of prayer without ceasing, I pray my way through each day in a variety of ways. The foundation of my prayer life is daily zazen. This silent wordless prayer provides a depth of stillness and presence that reverberates in subtle and profound ways throughout the rest of the day. The discipline and commitment to show up on the meditation cushion every day is itself a prayer to be open to God's will and presence in my life. Each week I meditate with New River Zen Community members on Wednesday evening and Sunday afternoon, and I attend church Sunday morning to pray with the Christian community. Each day I pray the Lord's Prayer and pray for family, friends, people everywhere, and the environment. At times during the day I intentionally practice mindfulness, such as when I am driving. I pay attention to just driving and don't get lost in doing other things like eating, drinking, talking on the phone, or planning my day. When I do certain repetitive tasks like sewing, I am mindful of each stitch. Each stitch is a prayer of love for the person who will wear the garment. When writing, I consider it a spiritual practice or prayer and open my whole mind, heart, and senses to the creative act.

One of my favorite prayer times each day is when I take a walk outside for exercise. I simply walk. Nonduality is experienced in *just this* walking. There is a shift from doing prayer to being prayer.

In one particular Zen koan, "A monk asked Ummon, 'What will it be when trees wither and leaves fall?' Ummon said, 'You embody the golden breeze'" (Sekida 2005, 218). Trees withered and leaves falling refer to death of the ego. When we transcend the sense of a separate self and the ego no longer dominates, how do we live and pray? We embody the golden breeze. Living fully awake and aware each moment without separation is prayer without ceasing.

> Everything is a prayer
> The tall pine against the wintery sky
> The oak tree holding onto sparse brown leaves
> Bare trees like black lace along the horizon
> Each shiny dark green magnolia leaf
> The cat walking along the top of the fence rail
> Houses, lampposts, sidewalks, and streets
> The silence of students taking an exam
> Each stroke on my keyboard, tap, tap, tap
> I am a prayer
> Each step
> Each breath
> Each a prayer
> Life itself a prayer
> Unceasing prayer
> Now and forevermore.

Part V

Embodying Loving Action

33

Ethics, Morality, Civility

Zen with its precepts and Christianity with its commandments both contribute to ethical behavior in the world. However, as Yamada Roshi notes, both Zen and Christianity do more than promote ethical principles based on reason and philosophy alone; they provide a foundation or moral basis for treating others with dignity and equality in the eyes of the law (Yamada 2015, 7–8). Zen leads to the direct experience that you and everyone else are manifestations of ultimate reality and thus are one. Moral behavior flows from this realization. Jesus taught that we are all sons and daughters of God. We are all made in God's image and likeness, and in this we are all worthy of dignity, justice, and love. This is the wellspring of morality.

In recent decades, there has been increased emphasis in Buddhist circles on engaged Buddhism, and rightly so. Christianity, since its beginning, has emphasized engaged social action, especially on behalf of those who are marginalized and oppressed. It is essential for the social action of Buddhists and Christians alike to remain deeply rooted in the wisdom of their respective traditions. For the Buddhist, compassionate action flows from the wisdom gained through meditation that you and the other are one. For the Christian, compassionate action flows from the love of God, of which you are a manifestation. You and your brothers and sisters, including those who are least in the eyes of the world, are one. Ultimate reality or God manifesting in the world provides the context and intimacy that motivate and sustain compassionate action.

Our culture today is besieged by incivility, divisiveness, and culture wars. There is a constant barrage of hostility on television, on the Internet, and in person. Many of the same people preaching love, compassion, and nonduality are lost in us-vs.-them battles hurling insults back and forth. People on both sides are often self-righteous, claiming the moral high ground, and being utterly intolerant of views other than their own. Meanwhile, there are many people in the middle, but their voices are not heard or respected amid the din. Where is the middle way? What can unite us to respect differences and find common ground?

The middle way is not mediocre; it is elegantly balanced. We express our opinions but do not cling to them or identify with them. We don't hit other people over the head with them. We listen to the opinions of others and are open to new ideas and information that may modify our own opinions. We recognize that opinions change and evolve—our own opinions and the opinions of others, if we don't dig in our heels and cling to extremes. Buddhist precepts urge us not to praise self or blame others (Dharma Rain Zen Center 2012, 41). Jesus urges us to love one another. If we embrace these teachings and the oneness from which they arise, we can truly listen to each other and walk the middle way together.

Scott, a member of New River Zen Community, told me that his wife, Gail, who died two years earlier, spoke eloquently at a city council meeting in Beckley, West Virginia, in 2014 in favor of the LGBTQ community's efforts to get the city council to amend their human rights ordinance to outlaw housing and employment discrimination against LGBTQ people. Gail was the only person who spoke in favor of the amendment because a large group of people from local fundamentalist churches filled up all the seats and spoke vigorously against it. The city council tabled the proposed amendment at that time. By 2019 the political climate in Beckley had changed, and the city council held two public hearings before voting on the same amendment. Scott was asked by the LGBTQ community to speak in favor of the amendment in Gail's stead, which he did. This time, many people, including Scott and a small community of Christians in the area who supported the amendment, spoke in favor of it. Although the amendment passed, Scott said that it was a painful experience to hear the outpouring of hatred and fear from the fundamentalist Christian community. Fortunately, he was comforted by an encouraging talk he had with a local Episcopalian priest after the meeting.

I have been at many meetings and gatherings where people on the left wing of the political spectrum have been equally hostile, making frequent negative comments about the intelligence or appearance of right-wing politicians and their spouses and children. Most disconcerting about this behavior is that people do not seem to be aware that many people in the room do not agree with them and that they are creating an uncomfortable environment in which to conduct the business of the meeting or to enjoy the fun of the gathering. This is beyond awkward; rather than drawing people in to support their causes, the incivility drives people away. Ken Wilber (2017b) has taken a lead in identifying the problem with this behavior, and in suggesting a way forward. Rather than being identified with only their own liberal or pluralistic level of development, Wilber suggests that they learn and grow to the integral level of development where they are able to incorporate beneficial values and viewpoints from all the different levels of human development.

Psychologist Jonathan Haidt (2012) also sheds light on the topic of divisiveness in religion and politics. His research found that people on the left tend to base their moral decisions primarily on three factors: care/harm, liberty/oppression, and fairness/cheating. People on the right base their moral decisions on six factors: care/harm, liberty/oppression, fairness/cheating, loyalty/betrayal, authority/subversion, and sanctity/degradation. In addition, there is a difference in how the left and right view fairness, with the left viewing fairness as equality, and the right factoring proportionality into the determination of fairness. Proportionality is the view that the person who does more work deserves more of the rewards of the labor. Understanding how people make moral decisions rather than simply declaring your own views superior is important. Appreciation of differences helps us work together to meet the many needs of the people and the planet.

Divisions within religious traditions are as great as divisions between different religious traditions, with new denominations and sects splintering off on an ongoing basis. Interspiritual practice is a way to transcend religious boundaries and celebrate our fundamental oneness as human beings sharing a home on planet Earth. We are here to love and care for one another and for the earth. Often, we do not agree on how best to do this, but we can move forward toward this goal by embodying love, care, and respect in the way we express our differences.

Sometimes silence unites. I have been at meetings and gatherings that begin with a period of silent meditation. Sitting in silence together, each person can open to that which is one's highest reality or ultimate concern. In this, there is a sense of oneness and our common humanity. Often at meetings that include this practice, people are better able to listen to each other with an open heart, the discourse is more profound, and people tend to be more unified toward finding solutions to relieve suffering, rather than finding fault.

34

Reverence

Reverence is the sense that human life and all creation are sacred because they are manifestations of ultimate reality or God. Our ability to treat each other, the earth, and all beings with love, care, and respect is rooted in our sense of the sacredness of all life. The sense of the sacred is gift or grace. It is feeling God's presence in us, around us, and as us. Meditation is a way to be fully present and open to the sacred. Sitting in silence with your awareness and senses open, and your energy not dissipated in thought, your perception becomes more subtle and refined. In this refined open awareness, the boundaries between inside and outside, self and other, subject and object dissolve. You see that there is one ultimate reality, one God, taking many forms. You experience that you are sacred, as is everything in the whole universe.

Reverence can be expressed toward the transcendent and the immanent God, or in Zen terms, toward the absolute and the relative. In church, we bow our heads in prayer to God, sing hymns of praise, and share in Holy Communion. In the zendo and Zen temple, we bow upon entering this sacred space, ring the bell, chant sutras, offer incense to honor Buddha and ancestors, and meditate in silence. These shared rituals and practices express our reverence for God or ultimate reality. They also express reverence for each other as manifestations of God or ultimate reality and as a sacred community.

Although church, zendo, temple, synagogue, kiva, and mosque are recognized as sacred places, actually each and every place, wherever you are at this moment, is a sacred place. A verse in *The Record of Transmitting the Light* reads,

> Know that in a remote place in a cloud-covered valley,
> There is still a sacred pine that passes through the chill of the
>   ages. (Cook 2003, 35)

The remote place is right here. The sacred pine is ultimate reality manifesting in you. All the ages are present in this moment. The sacred transcends space and time, yet manifests in each person, place, time, thing, action, and situation. Everything is sacred. When we recognize this, we treat each moment of life as sacred, as a sacred opportunity not to be missed. We embrace it and live it fully.

Zen offers many precise and careful gestures to express devotion, honor, and reverence in the zendo. The zendo is immaculate, with shoes carefully lined up outside the door. The floors and walkways are meticulously swept. The flowers are artfully arranged. There is no clutter. This attention to detail and orderliness is an expression of reverence for ultimate reality and for everything in the environment. It cultivates reverence and our ability to give this same careful attention to one another in daily life.

While in Japan, my husband and I took the bullet train from Tokyo to Kyoto to visit a friend at Hanazono University and to visit Zen temples. When the attendant entered the train car with the snack cart, she stopped and bowed to all the passengers before she began serving the snacks. This lovely gesture that communicated respect and civility demonstrates an attitude that is important for all workers to communicate to their clients. It reinforces a positive attitude toward the value of your work and respect for the people you serve. It is also a sign of respect and civility for clients to say thank you to those who provide the services they receive. Reverence and civility can be experienced and expressed through a bow in some cultures and in other cultures through a simple smile, greeting, handshake, or statement of thanks.

When my friend Karolyn's husband, Clarence, died, I attended his funeral. Clarence was a pilot in the air force for twenty years, including service during the Vietnam War. When he retired from his career in the military, he returned to Blacksburg, Virginia, the town where he grew up, and raised cattle on his farm. I chatted with Clarence in the grocery store a few days before he died. He was tall and dignified in his jeans, boots, and cowboy hat. He looked like the picture of health, and I thought, *That's how I want to be when I'm in my eighties*. At his funeral, they had a three-volley salute and a special ceremony presenting the flag to his wife. The reverence and the precise gestures and movements with which the flag was carefully folded and presented paid honor and tribute to the sacrifices he made to serve his country. It reminded me of the precise gestures and movements in Zen ceremonies. It also reminded me of the way the Navajo people honor their warriors, always having them walk first, carrying the flag in the parades at the powwows. Reverence is a sign of gratitude and respect that not only honors the one who served but also binds the community together, affirming what is honorable and valuable in our lives.

I gave birth to our daughter in Flagstaff, Arizona, at the foot of the San Francisco Peaks. We often gazed up at the majesty of the snow-capped peaks as we took our infant daughter for walks around town. The San Francisco Peaks are one of the four sacred mountains of the Navajo people that mark the northern, southern, eastern, and western boundaries of their land. We are one with the mountains and land, and it is essential in these days of impending ecological crises that we nurture our reverence for the land and realize that all mountains are sacred, all rivers and streams are sacred, and the air we breathe is sacred too. Realization of the sacredness of the land, waters, and sky is more than recognizing our dependence on them. It is directly experiencing oneness with them. This experience inspires and motivates us to take the actions needed every day to honor and protect them.

Now we live in Virginia between the Blue Ridge Mountains and the Jefferson National Forest. Often, we hike on the nearby

Appalachian Trail. Trail etiquette calls for leaving the area you hike through undisturbed and as pristine as when you arrived. This is in keeping with my early training as a Girl Scout, to carry out all trash that you took into the forest with you, leaving no trace. Experiencing nature firsthand, from the magnificence of the mountains and waterfalls to the delicate beauty of each trillium and rhododendron blossom, is awe-inspiring. One day, I sat on a log and watched gray lizards scurry about like tiny dinosaurs. Spending time in the woods, breathing fresh air, surrounded by all that is natural rather than made by humans, is our birthright. It connects us with something much larger than ourselves. Reverence for nature makes us want to conserve these sacred places so that those who come after us will have this awe-inspiring opportunity—an integral part of what it is to be fully human on this earth.

We experience and express reverence at times of birth and death and during other major life transitions, like weddings and graduations. We experience reverence in the face of beauty and in the face of suffering. Reverence includes and transcends religion, and it touches the heart of what being a decent human being entails. Reverence makes us want to bow down to that which is greater, makes us want to do better, makes us want to reduce suffering, and gives us the energy and vision to work to make the world a better place for everyone now, and for all those who will be born in the future.

35

Humility

Being humble means that you are down to earth, respectful, and kind, not lording your knowledge, wealth, or status over others. You are not arrogant, conceited, or standoffish. You are not egotistical, narcissistic, or pretentious. Comfort and joy come from being around a person who is genuinely humble. The person with true humility is natural and original, with no image to maintain. Being around a person with humility frees you to be who you are, and by example, calls forth your best.

In Zen, humility flows from the deep experience that ultimate reality is inconceivable, and as a manifestation of ultimate reality you too are inconceivable. Coming face-to-face with this type of "not knowing" is both awe-inspiring and humbling. It is liberating even as it leads us to take on the yoke of boundless compassion for self and others.

The following is a well-known koan in Gerry Wick's *The Book of Equanimity* about an encounter between Zen Master Jizo and a monk named Hogen who was on pilgrimage to various Zen monasteries in ancient China:

> Master Jizo asked Hogen, "Where have you come from?" "I pilgrimage aimlessly," replied Hogen. "What is the matter of your pilgrimage?" asked Jizo. "I don't know," replied Hogen. "Not knowing is the most intimate," remarked Jizo. At that, Hogen experienced great enlightenment. (Wick 2005, 63)

"Not knowing" in this context does not mean ignorance or not knowing the answer to a question in the ordinary sense. It refers to a direct encounter with ultimate reality, which is utterly inconceivable. This encounter comes when we let go of all thoughts, concepts, and images; everything we know or think we know; and especially what the ego or separate self wants most to hold onto, its ideas about itself and its control over life. When we let go of all that baggage, we open to something larger than the small, separate self and experience intimacy with the inconceivable. Life becomes fresh, new, and incredibly precious. We step forward into life with deep humility, love, and kindness.

In the Zen tradition, when we work on a koan, we meet with the Zen teacher privately to present our insight into the koan. This is not a verbal explanation or discussion of the meaning of the koan. The Zen student demonstrates or embodies the koan in some way.

Jesus demonstrated humility for his disciples, and for all of us, as Passover was approaching and his death was impending. He stood up from the table where he was dining with his disciples, took off his robe, got a towel, and poured water into a basin. Then he washed the feet of his disciples and dried them with the towel. When he was finished, he said, "So if I, your Lord and Teacher, have washed your feet, you also ought to wash one another's feet. For I have set you an example, that you should do as I have done for you" (John 13:15–16).

Jesus is showing us that although humans divide people and tasks into high and low, worthy and unworthy, God's view transcends division. No person or work is considered lowly, and no person is too lofty to do the most menial task. Each task or act can be done with great love, respect, and dignity. Jesus turns worldly views upside down when he says, "So the last will be first, and the first will be last" (Matt. 20:16). He tells us, "Whoever wishes to be great among you must be your servant" (Matt. 20:26).

We hear these teachings echoed in the Zen koan that says, "Even Shakyamuni and Maitreya are servants of that one. Just tell me, who is that one?" (Yamada 1990, 212). Shakyamuni Buddha is the historical Buddha, and Maitreya is a buddha who will come in the future. This koan points us toward the direct experience of ultimate reality and the experience that ultimate reality is manifesting in every person. When we serve others, we serve that one. There is nobody too lofty to serve others, and there is nobody too lowly to be served by others. Nonduality transcends dualistic divisions like high and low or server and served. All are manifestations of that one.

In his parable of the Lowest Seat, Jesus teaches us to be humble. He suggests that when we go to a wedding banquet, we should not sit in the seat of honor because, if someone more important comes after we arrive, the host will have to ask us to move to a lower seat, and that would be embarrassing. Instead we should sit in the lowest seat and then, when the other guests have been seated, the host may ask us to move to a higher seat, and that would bring us honor. Jesus says, "For all who exalt themselves will be humbled, and those who humble themselves will be honored" (Mark 10:43).

This is in keeping with the Zen precept that tells us not to put ourselves forward or put others down. We never want to elevate ourselves by putting others down, for this has the opposite effect. It reveals and reinforces our weaker tendencies. It brings us all down. We are ultimately one, and we rise and fall together. In college I had an education professor who told the class, "Never put a student down; the world will do this soon enough." Those words rang true to me. I remembered them and took them to heart through all my years as an educator.

Zen Master Linji once said,

> Beyond the red-meatball [mind] there is the one true *person* [true mind or buddha nature] who can't be ranked. [I.e., who does not belong to the "buddha" ranking and does not belong to the "sentient being" ranking.] [That true *person*/true mind] is constantly exiting and entering

from the face-gates of all of you people/persons [like the
dazzling rays of light emitted from the face-gate of a bud-
dha]. Those who have not seen with their own eyes—look!
Look! (Broughton & Watanabe 2013, 32)

The *red-meatball mind* can be interpreted as the functioning of our physical body and brain. *Face-gate* refers to a person's
mouth, or more broadly all the holes in our skull, including the
mouth, eyes, ears, and nostrils through which we interact and
communicate with the world around us. Inconceivable ultimate
reality manifesting in each of us is our true identity, the true person. The true person cannot be ranked high or low. It transcends
rank completely. In Zen, the true person is called the true person
with no rank. When you see this for yourself, you realize that you
are the person of no rank, and so is everyone else. This realization
is dazzling and gives rise to true humility.

When we have a Zen sesshin, we have a list posted so that
each member can sign up for two jobs, such as preparing a meal,
cleaning up after a meal, cleaning the zendo, cleaning bathrooms,
ringing the wake-up bell, taking out the trash and recycling, and
cleaning up at the end of sesshin. Mostly, Zen centers' jobs are
assigned, and over time, members rotate through doing all of
the jobs involved in keeping a Zen center maintained. Similarly,
churches' members have an opportunity once a year to sign up
to share their time and talents with the church community doing
various jobs such as maintaining the grounds, cooking for sick or
grieving members, helping in the office, teaching Sunday school,
singing in the choir, community outreach, and cleaning up after
potluck dinners. No church or Zen center can run smoothly
unless people volunteer to do all these different jobs. Volunteer-
ing, and the careful completion of these tasks, is a concrete expression of our insight, humility, and willingness to be servants to one
another. Often, it is in our service to one another that we make
lasting friendships.

At one sesshin, I was assigned, along with Ray Cecetti and Merle Kodo Boyd, to sweep the zendo each day. The zendo was in a picturesque but very dusty 150-year-old barn. Working in silence each morning, the three of us took all the mats and cushions out on the lawn and shook them out. Next, we earnestly swept the wide, weathered planks of the barn floor, trying not to laugh as we stirred up huge clouds of dust. Then we completed our humble task by putting the mats and cushions back into neat rows. To this day I feel a closeness with my two barn-sweeping companions, and it still makes me laugh every time I think of it.

36

Joy

Joy pervades the whole universe and you and me. It is enduring and deeper than happiness, which comes and goes. If you are too intent on seeking happiness, you may miss joy. Joy does not depend on momentary pleasures. It does not depend on things. Joy is present even amid sadness. The realization of your identity as a manifestation of God or ultimate reality brings great joy—vast, subtle, and infinite. There is a line in the Zen chant "Great Vows for All" that Bernie Glassman translated as "Always present, but rarely perceived" that can be used to describe joy. Joy is always present, but it is usually covered over with too many layers of thought and conditioning to be clearly perceived. Our hearts are often closed to its presence. That is why we need to sit in silent meditation each day, letting go of thoughts and conditioning, to open mind, heart, and every cell in the body to abiding joy.

Jesus said, "As the Father has loved me, so have I loved you; abide in my love. . . . I have said these things to you so that my joy may be in you, and that your joy may be complete" (John 15:9, 11). Jesus reveals God's love for us and the joy that flows from abiding in God's love. God's love and joy are infinite and unbounded, and we are manifestations of this infinite love and joy that we are called to share with one another. In this our joy is complete.

A Zen koan says, "Seijo and her soul are separated; which one is the true Seijo?" (Yamada 1990, 169). Seijo was a well-known tale at the time this koan took place in ancient China. When she was a child, Seijo played with her cousin Ocho, and when they got older, they fell in love with each other. In their culture, marriages were arranged by the parents, and Seijo's father did not select Ocho to be Seijo's husband. Before Seijo was married off to someone else, Seijo and Ocho ran away to a distant village and secretly got married. Although they had a happy life together raising their two children, one day they confided to each other that they were homesick. They decided to return home and seek Seijo's father's forgiveness. When they arrived home, Seijo and the children remained in the boat by the riverbank while Ocho went to talk with Seijo's father. When Seijo's father answered the door, he greeted Ocho warmly and told him that Seijo became ill many years ago when he left town, and she has been sick in bed ever since. Ocho told the father that was impossible because Seijo went with him to a distant village and he bid her father to come with him down to the boat to see her and meet his grandchildren. As the two men headed for the boat, they saw the Seijo who had been sick in bed all these years and the Seijo who was a young mother married to Ocho walk across the lawn toward each other and merge into one Seijo. Not only was the family joyfully reunited, but—and the main point of this koan—Seijo and her soul were no longer separate. Her joy was complete.

When you feel separate from ultimate reality or God, there is a longing, or a type of homesickness, because you are separate from who you are deep down. A phrase in Zen states, "Returning to your original dwelling place." When you awaken to who you are, by seeing through the illusion that you are a separate isolated self, you experience your true identity as a manifestation of ultimate reality or God. In this realization, there is a sense of great joy, a homecoming. You realize that your original dwelling place is right here, wherever you are. The whole universe is your home.

Nagarjuna and his successor, Kanadeva, were Zen ancestors in India in the second century. When Kanadeva had a meeting with Nagarjuna to become his follower, Nagarjuna had a bowl of water placed before Kanadeva. Kanadeva thrust a needle into the water and presented it to Nagarjuna. It says, "They met each other and joyfully realized that they were of like minds" (Cook 2003, 91). The clear water is like the emptiness and transparency of the absolute; the needle moves through it without resistance, yet it can be distinguished shining in the bottom of the bowl. The water and the needle are not one and not two. It is wonderful to imagine these two great minds meeting joyfully—Nagarjuna and Kanadeva sharing both their oneness of mind and their differences as two unique individuals meeting face-to-face and mind to mind.

In his book *Surprised by Joy*, C. S. Lewis describes his step-by-step transition over the years from being an atheist, to an idealist who believed in the Absolute, to a theist, and finally to a Christian. He said of the Absolute, "We have, so to speak, a root in the Absolute, which is utter reality. And that is why we experience Joy: we yearn, rightly, for that unity which we can never reach except by ceasing to be the separate phenomenal beings called 'we'" (Lewis 1955, 221–22). Lewis called the Absolute "the naked Other, imageless (though our imagination salutes it with a hundred images), unknown, undefined, desired" (1955, 221). He subsequently found that joy had been pointing him toward a relationship with God and with God's incarnation in Jesus Christ.

The Apostle Paul includes joy as one of the fruits of the Spirit, along with love, peace, patience, kindness, generosity, faithfulness, gentleness, and self-control (see Gal. 5:22–23). Opening your heart to the guidance of the Holy Spirit, and living accordingly, yields joy in your own life, a joy that overflows to those around you. A proverb says, "A cheerful heart is good medicine, but a downcast spirit dries up the bones" (Prov. 17:22). Joy is a powerful medicine that brings healing and wholeness to body, mind, and spirit.

In Buddhism, empathetic joy is one of the four immeasurables, along with loving-kindness, compassion, and equanimity (Wallace 2010). Empathetic joy is being joyful for the well-being and joy of others. We often think of expressing empathy when someone is having a hard time, but it is also important to express empathy regarding another's joy. We share with others our aware-ness of their joy and express that we are happy for them. Rather than being envious when others experience good fortune and joy in their lives, we are happy with and for them. Their joy brings us joy, and in this way, joy is multiplied. We develop a pattern of joy in life, rather than a pattern of discontent or envy.

We are each blessed with many simple joys every day. We do not need to manufacture joy; just notice it and appreciate it when it comes our way. This morning, standing at the kitchen sink washing strawberries to put on my cereal, bright sunlight flooded through the window, shining through the water flowing from the faucet, turning it into a stream of sparkles. The droplets of water rolling off my hands looked like a cascade of diamonds. The daz-zling light was as delicious as the breakfast. Joy begets joy.

37

Freedom

I am incredibly grateful to live in a time and place in which we have unprecedented freedom. We have access to the knowledge and wisdom of all the cultures and religious traditions of the world. We are free to explore and choose from among them those aspects that resonate with us most deeply, nourish us, breathe new life into us, and liberate us.

Zazen is a practice that liberates the human spirit. You sit down and let go of all that is weighing you down and boxing you in. You let go of thoughts, theories, and your expectations of how the world should be or how you should be. Zazen is not a self-improvement project. It is seeing beyond the sense of a separate self to experience that you are a manifestation of unbounded ultimate reality or God. Zazen is opening to what you already are. You sit, just as you are, awake and present to life just as it is right now.

There is a Zen koan in which "Zen Master Dayi bowed to Great Master Jianzhi and said, 'I beg the priest in his great compassion to give me the teaching of liberation.' The Patriarch replied, 'Who is binding you?'" (Cook 2003, 161). On a psychological level, there is much to learn from working with this koan. Sitting in zazen, we see and feel the tangle of thoughts and emotions that arise. Sitting silent and still, we can see how we bind ourselves with our likes and dislikes, expectations of ourselves and others, our perceived victories and disappointments, and our constant mental commentary on life. In letting go of all this, we experience the possibility of stepping out of this web of thoughts and emotions into life itself. Life liberates us if we are open to it in all its vastness and variety.

It is also possible to open completely to the realization of emptiness or ultimate reality, which transcends space and time. You experience firsthand emptiness or ultimate reality taking form in you and me and in everything in the universe. This realization of who you are liberates you from all sense of separation from ultimate reality or God, all separation between you and others, all separation from the earth and all beings, and all separation from the moon and the sky and the stars. This liberation is beyond your wildest imagination. It is inconceivable freedom.

With this insight, the chains of life and death are broken. As earthlings, we are born, we live, and we will die at some time, but in our oneness with ultimate reality and the whole universe, we transcend life and death, form and emptiness, now and then, bondage and liberation, heaven and earth, this and that. We do this here and now by living with vitality, presence, freedom, and unity with all life.

In Christianity, we are liberated by God's boundless love. Preaching in the synagogue in Nazareth, Jesus read the words of the prophet Isaiah: "The spirit of the Lord is upon me, because he has anointed me to bring good news to the poor. He sent me to proclaim release to the captives and recovery of sight to the blind, to let the oppressed go free, to proclaim the year of the Lord's favor" (Luke 4:18–19). The year of the Lord's favor is right now. God blesses us with boundless love. As a manifestation of God or ultimate reality we *are* God's boundless love. Love liberates us from the sin of separation from God, others, and all creation. Freed from the bondage of selfishness, we are no longer poor, bound, blind, or oppressed by our hearts of stone. God says, "A new heart I will give you, and a new spirit I will put within you; I will remove from your body the heart of stone and give you a heart of flesh" (Ezek. 36:26). We are freed to relate to others, the earth, and all beings with boundless love and compassion.

With great freedom comes great responsibility to live in accord with your insight and to work for the freedom of all people everywhere. Transcending the sense of a separate self, thereby realizing your oneness with ultimate reality and all creation, allows you to draw on boundless energy and love. However, the scope of this endeavor, to let freedom ring everywhere on earth, calls for both individual awakening and people working together in groups to change hearts, minds, and systems. We need to freely cross cultural, religious, political, and national boundaries to join hand in hand to establish freedom for all.

In the meantime, it is helpful to experience freedom even amid structures, systems, and the necessities of life that seem to bind us. A human body demands that we meet its needs for oxygen, water, food, elimination, and shelter from extremes of weather. As a member of a family, we are bound by love to work to meet our family's basic needs. Every job, regardless of how perfect it seems, constrains us in some way. In this sense, we never have complete freedom in this world, yet we can be free within our circumstances by accepting life just as it is and by accepting the truth of who we are in both an unbounded absolute and limited relative sense.

When you sit in zazen, you do not move even an inch from life as it is in the present moment. If you can't find freedom right here on this three-foot mat, where will you find it? The same is true in daily life. No matter what is happening, if you can't be free right here in the midst of life as it is, where will you experience freedom? Zazen is a way to develop this capacity and see for yourself that freedom is so much more than the absence of bondage.

What are you freed from, and what are you freed to see, do, and be? Once a monk asked Zen Master Nansen, "'What is the Dharma which has never been preached to the people?' Nansen said, 'This is not mind; this is not Buddha; this is not a thing'" (Yamada 1990, 134). Zen frees you from being dominated by things and the desire for things. It frees you from viewing yourself as a thing or another person as a thing or possession. Zen frees you from being dominated by thoughts, emotions, or mind. It frees you from thinking that mind, formlessness, or emptiness is something to grasp or cling to. Form and formless, mind and matter, emptiness and fullness are not separate. Zen liberates us from separation. It liberates us to see for ourselves the undivided wholeness of life. In this, we are liberated to live life fully moment by moment—*just this*!

Jesus said, "If you continue in my word, you are truly my disciples; and you will know the truth and the truth will set you free" (John 8:31–32). For Jesus, the truth was his oneness with God and God's love. By his words and example, he taught us to love God and one another. Jesus said, "If the Son makes you free, you will be free indeed" (John 8:36). We are liberated by walking the path of love each day through life's many twists and turns.

38

Love One Another

After Bernie Glassman had a stroke in 2016 he experienced paralysis, along with many other health problems. He worked hard to rehabilitate himself, but physical deficits and discomfort remained, curtailing his usual travels and activities. During a videoconference with his successors, someone asked him what he had left to live for. According to his wife, Eve, Bernie replied, "Love" (Burke 2018, 10).

Shortly before his betrayal and death, Jesus said to his disciples, "I give you a new commandment, that you love one another. Just as I have loved you, you also should love one another" (John 13:34–35). This commandment is a tremendous challenge, but loving one another becomes possible when you experience that you and your family members, neighbors, and coworkers are one in God or ultimate reality. Seeing through God's eyes enables you to love yourself and others as you strive to live a life of love. Loving one another is not a grim duty or obligation; it is a joyful expression of the oneness of life.

Jesus commands us not only to love one another but to love as he has loved us. Jesus's love for us is the boundless love of God. Experiencing and accepting God's love for us comes first. When we realize our true identity as a manifestation of ultimate reality or God, we see and feel that we are God's boundless love flowing out in all creation. When we love one another, we share what we are with others. We give to others from the boundless fountain of love that we are. There is no limit to love; the more we give, the more love there is in the world. We do all that we do with love—every act, small and grand.

As children, we learned the Golden Rule, "Do to others as you would have them do to you" (Luke 6:31). Through the ages, some version of this has been included in most of the world's religious traditions. These days, this rule has evolved into a version of the platinum rule that says, "Treat others as they would like to be treated." This highlights the fact that not all people view the world the way you do, and they may want to be treated differently than the way you want to be treated. This sensitivity to cultural and individual differences was emphasized in my nursing education from the start via Virginia Henderson's famous definition of nursing:

> Nursing is primarily assisting the individual (sick or well) in the performance of those activities contributing to health, or its recovery (or to a peaceful death), that he would perform unaided if he had the necessary strength, will, or knowledge. It is likewise the unique contribution of nursing to help the individual be independent of such assistance as soon as possible. (Harmer & Henderson 1960, 4)

This definition is not limited to nursing; it equally applies to anyone trying to love, care for, or assist another. It includes doing for others what they would do for themselves, if they could, and assisting in a way that does not promote or prolong dependence on the helper.

Loving another involves listening, so we get to know the other. We listen to what the other is experiencing and how he or she feels about it. We get to know what the other wants and does not want. Listening itself is a gift of love. The other person feels heard, known, accepted, respected, and valued. Meditation can be viewed as listening practice. We sit in silence, and rather than generating thoughts, words, and ideas, we let them all go, and we are present to whatever arises moment by moment without judgment. Meditation is practice in being open, alert, and receptive. It helps us be more present and open to others in daily life.

It is easy to be serene and feel love for people everywhere when we are sitting in silent meditation, but it is a challenge to embody love in our interactions with real people trying to agree on the best course of action to accomplish our mutual goals. In working with others, we put our equanimity and compassion to the test. Getting everyone to work together to accomplish a task requires listening to one another, respecting each person's unique gifts and input, and letting go of one's ego enough to be a team player. Working as a team, we can accomplish more together than we can on our own. Being part of a well-functioning team is one of life's greatest satisfactions, and in the process we grow to love one another.

Many people think of meditation as going within, but in zazen we sit with eyes, mind, and heart open, transcending inside and outside. We experience that we are not separate from ultimate reality, from others, or from the great earth and all beings. Zen Master Dogen taught that zazen *is* enlightenment. Similarly, loving action for others, the earth, and all beings *is* enlightenment.

Jesus urged us to feed the hungry, give drink to the thirsty, welcome the stranger, clothe the naked, care for the sick, and visit those in prison (see Matt. 25:35–37). He furthermore tried to help us realize his and our own oneness with people everywhere, especially those in need: "Just as you did it for the least of these . . . you did it to me" (Matt. 25:40).

There is a koan in which Zen Master Ummon says, "The world is vast and wide like this. Why do we put on our seven-panel robe at the sound of the bell?" (Yamada 1990, 79). The seven-panel robe, like Buddha's robe, is worn by Zen monks. When you look deeply into this koan you see that it is asking, "Why do you do anything that you do? Why do you respond to the bell, or to anything for that matter? Why do you sit in meditation and then go out to love and serve the world?" Not because you are required to, or to gain merit or get into heaven, but because ultimately that is what you are, that is what it is to be fully alive as a human being on this earth. You transcend *why*, and love responds with love.

I have often been moved by interspiritual practice to "see how they love one another" across centuries of traditional boundaries. Sitting together in silent meditation with people from all faiths and none, boundaries between Christian, Jew, Muslim, Buddhist, and secular humanist are transcended. You don't become the other, but you realize you and the other are one. You love others, grieving their sorrows and celebrating their joys. You appreciate your common humanity as well as your differences. At interfaith events and sesshin that I attended, it always touched my heart to see Rabbi Don Singer, Father Robert Kennedy, and Roshi Bernie Glassman relate to one another as brothers. One of the most memorable occasions was a New Year's Eve sesshin in Connecticut. At midnight, we sat on our mats in a large circle meditating together while hearing the bell ring 108 times. Afterward, we celebrated the new year by sitting in silence as people, one at a time or as a couple, spontaneously sang songs from various spiritual traditions. It was amazing to hear all the different flavors of spirituality ring through the night and echo through the hall. There were Jewish songs, Christian Gregorian chant, Hindu chants, and Sufi songs. Charles and I sang a song we learned on the reservation many years earlier. Part in Navajo and part in English, it was about walking in beauty. The beauty and harmony of all these different traditions coming together in love was palpable. What a wonderful way to start the new year!

In both Zen and Christianity, talking about God and ultimate reality, and gaining wisdom from meditation and prayer, are not enough. The depth of our wisdom is reflected in our loving service to others. Often at the end of a Sunday service, the pastor, priest, or deacon says, "Go in peace to love and serve the world." This is where responding to the meditation bell and responding to the cries of the world are one: one love.

39

Work as a Gift

Zen is subtle and paradoxical, and at the same time simple, practical, and disciplined; that is what makes it so powerful. We sit silent and still, allowing the bodymind to settle so that we can experience the empty oneness of all things. Then we bring this clarity into daily life. We see empty oneness or ultimate reality manifesting in our every act—hearing, seeing, walking, eating, typing, building, cleaning, and healing. This is what Yamada Roshi calls *the fact* (Yamada 1990, 33), the seamless functioning of the whole. This is also called nonduality or *just this*.

In the zendo, someone is appointed to serve as head monk. The head monk makes sure the zendo is in order, handles all practical matters that arise in the zendo, and makes sure everyone maintains silence in the zendo and during breaks. Invariably, when you get a group of people together, some are too hot and some are too cold. The head monk opens and closes the windows or adjusts the thermostat to maintain an optimum temperature for the group. Nobody needs to give it any thought or get in an argument about it. We just give input to the head monk during a break and accept the common sense of the person in charge. This not only allows us to practice as a group in an orderly manner, it helps us learn to let go of our ego and selfish clinging by turning zendo matters over to someone else to decide in the group's best interests.

Zen Master Pai-chang, who lived in the eighth century in China, is credited with establishing the rules and daily schedule for Zen monasteries to balance zazen with the work needed to build and support the monastery. Previously, monks survived primarily by begging. Monks continued to beg for alms, as a spiritual practice, but the monasteries now met their basic needs through agriculture. Pai-chang is famous for saying, "A day without working is a day without eating" (Cleary 1978, 26). However, the value he placed on work went far beyond simply surviving.

During periods of work practice, Zen practitioners work in silence, except for brief questions or comments related to effective completion of the task at hand. Working in silence, you can feel the texture of the materials you are working with, whether it be fabric, food, earth, wood, or stone. You can feel the muscles of your body actively engage and release in the repetitive motion of raking, sweeping, cleaning, chopping, kneading, or ironing. Letting go of thoughts unrelated to the work, your mind clears, and your body is grounded in the earth and the activities of daily living. Working together you bond as a group and with all humanity who must work for a living. Assigned tasks rotate, so all members of the community gain practical skills—gardening, cooking, cleaning, doing laundry, building, and sewing. Members grow in competence, confidence, and common sense. The dignity of work is affirmed, no matter the task assigned.

In the following koan, Pai-chang helps us take a leap even further into the value of work:

> Yun-yen asked the master, "Every day there's hard work to do; who do you do it all for?" The master said, "There is someone who requires it." Yun-yen said, "Why not have him do it himself?" The master said, "He has no tools." (Cleary 1978, 26)

This koan helps us see that the work we do is a gift from, and for, that which is greater than the small, separate ego self. We don't work just for the rewards we gain from our labors such as money, material things, and status. We work from a sense of our identity as a manifestation of ultimate reality taking form in each of us and in the earth and all beings. Not only does "the one who requires it" have no tools, but "the one who requires it" has no hands but our hands. We work with the sense that our hands are Buddha's hands or Christ's hands in the world. Work is our gift to meet our own needs, and to reach out to love and serve others and the earth with whom we are one.

Last week at the end of the Sunday service, as I started to exit the sanctuary, a large banner hanging over the double doors at the front of the church caught my eye. In foot-tall letters it said, "Servants' Entrance." This was an excellent reminder and celebration of the work we are called to do in the world daily. It is a reminder to do our work with an attitude of selfless service rather than a self-serving attitude. With an attitude of selfless service, we do our work with love, kindness, and dignity. In this spirit, we put forth our best effort in whatever work we do, whether at home, in the workplace, or in the community.

When I saw this banner, it made me think of our usual Zen etiquette where we bow at the doorway before entering the zendo. Perhaps we should also start bowing toward the world as we exit the zendo doorway. This gesture would place equal emphasis on the sacredness of meditation in the zendo and on the sacredness of compassionate action in the world.

I could not have done the work I did as a nurse without both Christianity and Zen. From Christianity, I got the call to serve Christ in the form of the sick and the dying. Ironically, Zen helped me see and feel that I am Christ in the world doing the healing work.

Sometimes when I was getting ready to go off for a weekend or weeklong sesshin, and a coworker asked me where I was going, I would say, "To a Zen retreat." Often the coworker would reply something like, "Oh, have a great time and enjoy the peace and quiet. Get some rest. You deserve it." In my mind, I thought, *Little do you know that a Zen retreat is more like boot camp than a week of rest and relaxation.* A sesshin consists of a rigorous week or weekend of many meditation periods beginning before dawn and ending after dark, interspersed with work periods, chanting, meals, and brief breaks. All this is done together, with great attention, day and night.

From Zen, I got the discipline, stamina, and clarity to work long and hard as a nurse. Often working as a nurse in the neonatal intensive care unit, several high-risk babies would be born at the same time and the staff would be stretched thin. We worked for hours through the night on our feet with barely time to go to the bathroom and no time to break for a meal. With eyes and ears open, and all our equipment and supplies neatly stacked within arm's reach, we were ready to respond as a team to any emergency that arose. Each shift, one of us was assigned to check the crash cart and the transport box to be sure everything was in its place. After each crisis, we immediately replaced anything we had used to be sure we were ready, on a moment's notice, for the next situation. Amid all this, we worked with the utmost love for each infant and family. There was never a time that I witnessed any baby or family being discriminated against from receiving state-of-the-art care and our love. Nurses and doctors from many different faiths and none drew on their spiritual resources—along with their physical, emotional, and mental resources—to provide this level of care. This was interspiritual practice at its finest.

40

Expressing the Inconceivable

The inconceivable expresses itself in our very existence here on earth. We express the inconceivable in our being and in every breath we take. God or ultimate reality expresses itself in each of us in a unique way. While there are many factors, such as genetics, culture, nurture, and environment, that influence the range of choices available to each of us moment by moment, a wide array of choices remains for us to make in life. The most fundamental choice we make is to open to the inconceivable God or ultimate reality and express its unbounded love and compassion in all that we think, say, and do.

This choice begins with nurturing and developing yourself as the particular human being who you are. Many people misinterpret selflessness to mean that our energy and attention should go toward helping others and not toward meeting our own needs or toward developing our talents. However, our life and our talents are not our own; they are gifts to be used for the benefit of all. If we don't take care of ourselves and develop our talents, we will not have the energy or abilities needed to help others effectively.

Jesus told a parable about talents, which were different amounts of money that a master entrusted to his three servants, according to the ability of each. Two of the servants invested the money wisely and doubled the amount entrusted to them. The third hid his money in the ground for safekeeping. Later, the master returned. He was pleased with the work of the first two servants and said to each of them, "Well done, good and trustworthy servant . . . enter into the joy of your master" (Matt. 25:21). The master was not pleased with the third servant and chastised him for hiding, rather than wisely investing, the talent entrusted to him.

When we realize that our talents are gifts for the benefit of all, we embrace the responsibility to develop and use them wisely. This includes all our gifts, such as the gift of health. Whatever our level of health, we need to exercise, get enough sleep, eat nutritious food, and avoid mind-dulling alcohol and drugs in order to have the energy and vitality needed to care for others and the earth. It is important not to squander the life and health that have been given to us. Exercise is necessary to maintain health and should be joyful and invigorating, such as walking, running, swimming, yoga, or dancing, according to our own unique physiology and preferences. Likewise, eating well is one of life's greatest pleasures. It unites us with the seasons and the earth. On Mother's Day each year, I plant my small kitchen garden, which I can see from the window as I wash dishes. I plant tomatoes, greens, and herbs. There is nothing like the flavor and juiciness of a fresh homegrown tomato. A friend gave me a cement statue of Hotei Buddha, which stands in the corner of the garden presiding over the parsley. It makes me smile each time I look at it.

In order to develop your own talents, you need to reflect on what you are good at and what your passions are. Are you interested in cooking, health care, construction, computer science, writing, auto mechanics, engineering, religion, business, science, or the arts? What are your strengths and limitations? What contributions can you make for the well-being of the earth and all beings? The next step is to take advantage of whatever educational opportunities are available to you in your chosen field. This is how you multiply your talents to serve others and address the problems of our world. Our helping should be based not only on our spiritual insight but also on the best scientific knowledge available.

In my thirty-two years as a nurse educator, I was always amazed to see the growth of students over the course of their nursing studies and upon graduation to see them accept jobs in diverse settings such as emergency departments, intensive care units, neuro-trauma units, nursing homes, oncology units, and pediatric units. What was even more gratifying was to go to a hospital or clinic as a patient and receive outstanding care from nurses who were my students just a year or two earlier. I marvel at what a valuable resource they are to their communities.

Bernie Glassman and Rick Fields wrote a book titled *Instructions to the Cook* (1996) based on Zen Master Dogen's book by the same title. In it, they tell the well-known story of Dogen arriving in China after a perilous journey by sea from Japan. When the ship docks, Dogen meets an old monk who walked twelve miles to the ship to get some special mushrooms grown in Japan. The monk is the *tenzo*, or cook, at his monastery. Dogen invites the monk to spend the night so that they can talk about Zen, but the monk says he has to return to the monastery to get the food prepared for a special celebration the next day. Despite the urgings of Dogen to stay, the monk says that it is his responsibility to prepare the food for the monks, and despite his advanced age, he sets off to walk the twelve miles back to the monastery. The monk invites Dogen to visit him at the monastery; impressed with the monk's spirit and dedication, Dogen later follows up on this invitation. Bernie wrote an inscription in my copy of his book that says, "Ellen, please cook the Supreme Meal with all your wonderful ingredients. With all my love, Bernie." Like the monk in the story, and like Bernie, we need to use all the gifts and talents we are given in life to cook the Supreme Meal and lovingly serve others, the community, the earth, and all beings.

A contemplative practice such as Zen meditation is essential to experience that ultimate reality, oneself, others, and the world are not separate. The secular is sacred. Most of us today are lay practitioners—contemplatives in action. We do not live in monasteries. We live in the world and need to balance family responsibilities, full-time work, spiritual practice, and social action. Meditation is a way to find balance, to experience the oneness of life and the compassion that arises from this insight, and to regenerate and reenergize ourselves.

Social action needs to be rooted in wisdom and love. There are so many urgent problems at home and abroad, such as environmental degradation, starvation, disease, mental illness, addiction, war, and oppression. We each need to be engaged in finding creative solutions to these problems. Some social actions can be integrated into daily life, such as simplifying our lifestyle and reducing our consumption to preserve the environment. Many issues can be addressed by careful study and judicious voting. Some issues are best addressed by joining organizations that confront specific problems. However, we need to be selective so that we don't become overwhelmed, depressed, and exhausted. Join a favorite project or organization that is close to your heart, and don't try to do everything at once. It is essential in our social action that we don't become hostile, bitter, divisive, violent, and exhausted; that we don't put others down; and that we don't view people with opinions different from our own as the enemy. These attitudes and behaviors add to the problem rather than reducing suffering in the world. Social action is one aspect of being a contemplative in action, but so is time for contemplative practice. We need to find the middle way so that we don't burn out and harm ourselves and others while trying to help.

Matthew Fox notes that an integrated, balanced, and mature spirituality means "accepting the truth of ourselves as co-creators with God" (1983, 184). When you embrace the inconceivable, you realize that you are inconceivable, and that what you are capable of is also inconceivable. You unleash your creativity and open to infinite possibilities that can be brought to bear on addressing the problems of the world in unforeseen ways, always with an eye toward the bigger picture: God or ultimate reality.

41

Keep Going

There is no end to spiritual development and insight. Awakening is an ongoing, moment-by-moment process. That is why it is essential, from the start, to realize that the means and ends are one. Sitting in meditation and engaging in compassionate action *are* enlightenment. Each day, fresh and new, get up, meditate, and then go out to act in each circumstance that arises with love, enthusiasm, and deep joy. The inconceivable is boundless; there is no beginning and no end. Although God or ultimate reality is inconceivable, you can have transformative glimpses and intimate encounters with this great reality that expand your mind and heart beyond anything imaginable.

Jesus urges us to walk the path of love. In his life, he taught us, by example, to go to the garden, mountain, desert, or a room in your house to pray. Then he went out into the towns, synagogues, and hillsides to share the love of God through teaching, feeding, forgiving, liberating, and healing the people. We are to do likewise.

Jesus is often depicted as a shepherd carrying a lamb on his shoulders. In his parable of the Lost Sheep, he tells us that a shepherd cares about every one of his sheep. If even one of them gets lost, he leaves the ninety-nine and goes searching for the one who is lost. This is an image of Jesus living close to the earth and to the creatures of the earth. In Jesus's life and teachings, he reveals that God not only exists but that God cares for each and every one of us and for all the creatures of the earth. As human beings, created in the image and likeness of God, we are called to care for each other, all creatures, and the earth itself. To the extent we do this, we realize our full humanity and the glory of God.

Buddha is usually depicted sitting in the posture of meditation. Some Buddha paintings and sculptures show his hand extended downward touching the earth. When Buddha sat down under the Bodhi tree in meditation to awaken, he was taunted by Mara, the embodiment of unwholesome desires, who told him that it was no use trying to teach others about what he had experienced because no one would witness to the truth of what he was saying. In reply, Buddha touched the earth and said, "The earth is my witness." Buddha taught us that there is a way to end needless suffering by meditating and seeing beyond the sense of a separate self. We awaken to our true identity as a manifestation of ultimate reality. Such an awakening is accompanied by the spontaneous arising of compassion and love for others, the earth, and all beings from whom we are not separate.

In *The Record of Transmitting the Light*, Zen Master Keizan tells us, "On the basis of your diligence or lack of diligence, the Buddha either appears or does not appear. . . . Therefore, you must practice the Way at once and encounter your compassionate father promptly. Daily the old fellow Shakyamuni and you walk about, stand in place, sit, and lie down together, and you have words together without even a moment of separation" (Cook 2003, 35). Keizan urges us to be diligent in meditation every day. He tells us that if we are diligent, we will come face-to-face with ultimate reality and experience compassion for all.

In embracing the inconceivable, there is intimacy and boundless love. Nothing is excluded. We surrender to that which is utterly inconceivable, which is greater than we are, and which is inexhaustible. It brings great joy to encounter the inconceivable in meditation and in daily life in new ways each day. It never gets old. We humbly spend our time on earth embracing the inconceivable in each person we meet; in each situation, whether pleasant or painful; and in each plant, animal, rock, and star. We do our best to respond as a fully alive human being who loves and cares.

In writing about the interspiritual practice of Zen and Christianity, I am simply sharing the joy and insights I have experienced with those who may be interested in interspiritual practice. However, I cannot emphasize enough that the key word here is *practice*. The danger in reading a book like this is that you may think you understand what I am saying, but unless you actually meditate long and strong, with the guidance of an authorized Zen teacher, and with a *sangha* to support your practice, it is unlikely that you will go deep enough to experience the fruits of Zen practice. The same is true of walking the Christian path. The fruits of the Spirit do not come from reading alone. They come from study, prayer, spiritual direction, loving action, and participation in a Christian community. In my life I have focused on these two spiritual traditions because it is difficult to go deep enough into more than two traditions, and depth is of essence. So whatever spiritual paths you pursue, go deep and bring forth the gifts of those traditions to enrich your life and the lives of others.

Once Yakusan was sitting in meditation, and Zen Master Sekito asked him, "What are you doing there?" "I am doing nothing at all," said Yakusan. Sekito said, "You say you are doing nothing. What is it you are not doing?" Yakusan replied, "Even thousands of old Buddhas do not know." Sekito approved of Yakusan's answer (Sekida 2005, 263–64). Zen meditation is not about doing; it is about letting everything drop away so that you can clearly see what you already are. Along with thousands of old Buddhas, we too do not know. We embrace the inconceivable, which cannot be grasped with the intellect or expressed in words.

Both Zen and Christianity require you to let go of the ego completely and surrender to that which is greater than your furthest imagination. When you take this leap, you see that you are not separate from ultimate reality or God. You are not separate from your own true identity as a manifestation of ultimate reality or God. Ultimate reality or God is inconceivable, and so are you. You are not separate from other people, the earth, all beings, and the whole universe. In the realization of nonseparation or nonduality, boundless love and compassion arise. You are liberated to live as a decent, authentic, loving human being.

Works Cited

Akizuki, Ryomin. 1994. "The Common Ground for Buddhism and Christianity: A Basis for World Peace" Paper prepared for conference at Lasalle Haus Bad Schonbrunn, Switzerland.

Batchelor, Stephen. 2015. *After Buddhism: Rethinking the Dharma for a Secular Age*. New Haven, CT: Yale University Press.

Broughton, Jeffrey L., and Elise Yoko Watanbe, trans. 2013. *The Record of Linji*. New York: Oxford University Press.

Burke, Daniel. 2018, December 1. "An American Zen Master Has Died." CNN. https://www.cnn.com.

Cleary, Thomas, trans. 1978. *Sayings and Doings of Pai-chang*. Los Angeles: Center Publications.

Cleary, Thomas, and J. C. Cleary, trans. 2005. *The Blue Cliff Record*. Boston: Shambhala.

Conze, Edward. 1972. *Buddhist Wisdom Books: Containing the Diamond Sutra and the Heart Sutra*. New York: Harper & Row.

Cook, Francis Dojun, trans. 2003. *The Record of Transmitting the Light*. Boston: Wisdom.

Dharma Rain Zen Center. 2012. "Chant Book." https://dharma-rain.org.

Erdman, David V., ed. 1982. *The Complete Poetry and Prose of William Blake*. Berkeley: University of California Press.

Ferguson, Andrew. 2000. *Zen's Chinese Heritage*. Somerville, MA: Wisdom.

Fischer-Schreiber, Ingrid, Franz-Karl Ehrhard, and Michael S. Deiner. 1991. *The Shambhala Dictionary of Buddhism and Zen*. Translated by Michael H. Kohn. Boston: Shambhala.

Fox, Matthew. 1983. *Original Blessing*. New York: Jeremy P. Tarcher/Putnam.

Glassman, Bernard, and Rick Fields. 1996. *Instructions to the Cook*. New York: Bell Tower.

Haidt, Jonathan. 2012. *The Righteous Mind*. New York: Pantheon.

Haight, Roger. 2016. *Spiritual and Religious*. Maryknoll, NY: Orbis.

Harmer, Bertha, and Virginia Henderson. 1960. *Textbook of the Principles and Practice of Nursing*. 5th edition. New York: Macmillan.

Hixon, Lex. 1995. *Living Buddha Zen*. Burdett, NY: Larson.

Johnson, Elizabeth A. 2018. *Creation and the Cross*. Maryknoll, NY: Orbis.

Kapleau, Philip. 1989. *The Three Pillars of Zen*. 25th anniversary edition. New York: Doubleday.

Kavanaugh, Kieran, and Otilio Rodriguez, trans. 1979. *The Collected Works of St. John of the Cross*. Washington, DC: Institute of Carmelite Studies.

Kennedy, R. E. 2016, February 22. "A New Secular Way." *America*, 35–37.

Lewis, C. S. 1955. *Surprised by Joy*. New York: Harcourt, Brace, & World.

MacInnes, Elaine. 2007. *The Flowing Bridge*. Boston: Wisdom.

Maslow, Abraham H. 1970. *Motivation and Personality*. 2nd ed. New York: Harper & Row.

McGinn, Bernard. 1986. *Meister Eckhart: Teacher and Preacher*. New York: Paulist.

Morton, Michael. n.d. "Forgiveness and Three Powerful Truths." www.beliefnet.com.

————. *Getting Life*. 2014. New York: Simon & Schuster.

Neff, Kristin. 2011. *Self-Compassion*. New York: William Morrow.

Rogers, Murray, 2006. "Transcript of an Interview with the Rev. Murray Rogers on Swami Abhishiktananda" (interview by Christian Hackbarth-Johnson). https://dimmid.org.

Salzberg, Sharon. 2016, September 28. "Mindfulness Conference." Roanoke, Virginia.

Sasaki, Ruth Fuller. 2009. *The Record of Linji*. Edited by Thomas Yuho Kirchner. Translated by Ruth Fuller Sasaki. Honolulu: University of Hawaii Press.

Sekida, Katsuki, trans. 2005. *Two Zen Classics*. Boulder, CO: Shambhala.

Seligman, Martin E. P. 2002. *Authentic Happiness*. New York: Free Press.

Seo, Audrey Yoshiko. 2007. *Enso: Zen Circles of Enlightenment*. Boston: Weatherhill.

Shaku, Soen. 1906/1987. *Zen for Americans*. Translated by Daisetz Teitaro Suzuki. New York: Dorset.

Shaw, Anna Howard. 1915. *The Story of a Pioneer*. New York: Harper & Brothers.

Shibayama, Zenkei. 2000. *The Gateless Barrier*. Translated by Kudo Sumiko. Boston: Wisdom.

Siderits, Mark, and Shoryu Katsura. 2013. *Nagarjuna's Middle Way*. Boston: Wisdom.

Still Mind Zendo. n.d. "Chants." https://www.stillmindzendo.org.

Tang, Yi-Yuan, Britta K. Holzel, and Michael I. Posner. 2015. "The Neuroscience of Mindfulness Meditation." *Nature Reviews Neuroscience* 16, no. 4: 213–25.

Teasdale, Wayne. 1999. *The Mystic Heart*. Novato, CA: New World Library.

Thompson, William M. 1994. "'Distinct but Not Separate': Historical Research in the Study of Jesus and Christian Faith." *Horizons* 21, no. 1 (1994): 130–41. doi:10.1017/S0360966900027961.

Tolstoy, Leo. 1899. *Resurrection*. Translated by Louise Maude. New York: W. W. Norton.

Vermont Zen Center. 2008. "Morning Services."

Village Zendo. 2019. https://www.villagezendo.org.

Waddell, Norman, trans. 2000. *The Unborn: The Life and Teachings of Zen Master Bankei, 1622–1693*. New York: North Point.

Wallace, Alan B. 2010. *The Four Immeasurables*. Boston: Snow Lion.

Wick, Gerry Shishin. 2005. *The Book of Equanimity*. Boston: Wisdom.

Wilber, Ken. 1995. *Sex, Ecology, Spirituality*. Boston: Shambhala.

———. 2017a. *The Religion of Tomorrow*. Boulder, CO: Shambhala.

———. 2017b. *Trump and a Post-Truth World*. Boulder, CO: Shambhala.

Yamada, Koun. 1990. *Gateless Gate*. Tucson: University of Arizona Press.

———. 2015. *Zen: The Authentic Gate*. Somerville, MA: Wisdom.

Zen Peacemaker Order Service Book. 1997. Montague, MA: Peacemaker Circle International.

Index

197